AN UNFINISHED PORTRAIT

JOURNEYS AROUND MY MOTHER

MIRIAM FRANK

GIBSON SQUARE

I wish to dedicate this journey into my mother's life and our relationship to my two daughters, in my reverse role as mother.

To Rebekah and Anna, with my love.

And to my late publisher, Gary Pulsifer, who encouraged me to write it.

This edition published for the first time in 2017 by Gibson Square

UK   Tel: +44 (0)20 7096 1100
US   Tel: +1 646 216 9813

rights@gibsonsquare.com
www.gibsonsquare.com

ISBN 978-1783341238

Papers used by Gibson Square are natural, recyclable products made from wood grown in sustainable forests; inks used are vegetable based. Manufacturing conforms to ISO 14001, and is accredited to FSC and PEFC chain of custody schemes. Colour-printing is through a certified CarbonNeutral® company that offsets its CO2 emissions.

Printed by CPI.

Contents

Prologue

The soft squish of the shutter release joined the bustle in the forecourt of the depot. I balance the heavy camera with its powered zoom lens, focus on the painting, and press the button before the men carefully lift it and load it into the van with all the other works.

Each piece of work was to be recorded before making the journey. More than one hundred paintings, assorted portfolios bulging with drawings and other graphics, along with boxes full of books, prized letters, old photographs and other objects from his past to be shipped to Austria. My husband has sent for them in preparation for a retrospective exhibition and publication of his artwork in Salzburg, where in years past he directed the visual arts department at the *Internationale Sommerakademie* and he has returned to live.

One curious, unfinished portrait had suddenly emerged out of the pile of paintings being carted out, one by one, from the large cubicle along the narrow corridor on the second floor of the storage depot. They were tightly packed, front to front, and back to back, along with the many boxes, stacked one on top of the other, that contained my husband's personal belongings which he had left behind when our marriage broke up. I had moved them to this site for their safekeeping, close to my new apartment by the Thames.

I was surprised to see this portrait again after so many years; I had lost sight of it after he abandoned it and put it away. It brought back memories of my long silent sittings in the soft natural light of the studio, hemmed in amongst the various canvases at different stages of completion, untidy piles here and there of drawings, etchings, lithographs and all the other paraphernalia that had mounted up over the years, the tubes of oil paint spreading their faintly resinous odour lying on the floor before him in their every hue and colour as he would pick one after the other to squirt and mix and scrape on the broken piece of plate-glass he used as a palette. He had worked long and hard on the portrait over several months, when we were still together, all that time ago. I remember his battle with it – the huge concentration, effort and struggle – until he gave it up. Beaten. And yet, even so, he has captured something there.

The eyes... One is a green splodge of paint in preparation, I suspect, for the colours he was calculating to spread over it in the following sittings. The other eye stares back at me with all my life and being imprinted on it: the strengths and insights driven into me from all I have learnt and experienced in life look out of that eye straight back at me. Maybe it was the fiercely held back and firmly contained pain, mixed with a certain defiance, hovering somewhere in the back of that dark oblong patch that forms the pupil, that had stopped him in his tracks. Or possibly that deeply tormented and confused aspect of himself which he has also – as likely as not, unwittingly – worked into the eye, turning it into a mirror of our disturbed relationship over the years.

In the portrait's unfinished state, one eye remains frozen in its unformed, primeval state, forever waiting to be imprinted with all that is yet to come, while the other is alive and cognisant and has gathered a raw energy of its own. In its penetrating, unflinching gaze, I also see something of the tense, unresolved rift with my mother that underlay much of my life's tangled and intricate course; the eye's look appears to be imploring me to go back to the source, to dredge out the seeds of our misunderstandings and soothe the wounds – however unfinished may my journey remain.

Mediterranean Montage

The Cycladic island of Serifos

Here the sky soars into a deep unending blue dissolving into the receding void, over and beyond. The empty rocky landscape towers everywhere stark and craggy, and the sea stretches out into a sparkling crystalline aquamarine. Here and there, sporadic villages display their sunlit clusters of white cubes nestling on the side of a mountain, or looking down from the edge of a precipitous rock-face. The principal one, Chora, cascades from the top of a conical hill down towards the port like a shimmering white bridal veil.

Across the Aegean Sea, wars have been raging, one after another, from the start of human history. People have been fighting over their diverse ethnicities and religions, ancient and renewed rivalries and never-ending territorial disputes; for enforced control and subjugation, or an elusive freedom and choice in their lives.

The Bosnian war was in full swing when I first came here during the summer – staying in a house built from the ruins of three, single-roomed dwellings inside the walled hilltop of the Chora – at the turn of the millennium. The onslaught, now, is taking place in Syria. In between, other savage attacks and counterattacks have led to countless deaths, maimings, loss of families and homes, and heartrending suffering and devastation in the Middle Eastern and North African lands that rim the Mediterranean. Blind passions take hold and become entrenched, turning adversaries oblivious to each other's fundamental likeness, with the same basic needs, aspirations and desires: keeping alive the renewed cycle and never-ending waves of refugees leaving behind home and country, seeking survival and new lives in exile.

Here on this island – with its vast watery moat keeping at bay all that human confusion and animosity across the waves – I concentrate on my more immediate reality. In this tranquil spot, far removed from those timeless conflicts, I immerse myself instead in the stark, uncorrupted beauty all around me; I experience at close hand the raw elements of earth, rocks, sea and sky. And wind. A fierce, howling, unrelenting wind, indu-

View of Chora, in Serifos, the house in the top lefthand corner

bitably venting God's exasperation with us, as it gusts, shudders and blasts across the island. Sometimes for days and weeks on end. And when it finally subsides, the sun glows down softly, the air shines crystal clean and clear, the warmth glories in a gentle breeze, the peace perfect.

The house I come back to again and again here is a geometric play of chalky white thick stone walls cut into arched and rectangular openings between rooms creating a multi-leveled open space throughout, the light flooding in through the high skylight, glazed doors and windows heightening the manifold shades of white on the curved, straight and slanting surfaces. From where I sit, I also see the buff and olive tones of the mountains towering above the village, and the changing blues of the sky and the sea beyond.

Once, as I stood on my terrace, looking into the distance, I picked out large flying shapes moving onto the island from the sea. As they advanced slowly and gracefully towards me, I realised they were some kind of stork. It was early evening, and the day's clear bright light was starting to fade. By now these beautiful, long-legged, long-beaked creatures, with their massive flapping wings, were flying all around the neighbouring houses, alighting on the cables and flat roofs and discovered niches. They appeared to be looking for somewhere to break their flight for the night – wherever it was they were coming from or going to. One, to my enchantment, settled on my roof. By now it was dark. When I rose to look for them again in the early morning, they were all gone.

I was left wondering which home and country and skies and season they came from, and which entirely different ones they were flying to with such resolve.

The island is surrounded by beaches, some with the finest white sand, others more grainy and golden, or covered with pebbles of many colours, and the cerulean sea is crystal clear down to its light sandy floor alternating with darker patches of vegetation and marine life. One remote beach in the north of the island is spread with smoothly rounded white pebbles like sugared almonds; another on its western side, where iron abounds and was once mined, is scattered with knobbly, black, molten lumps of irregular forms and sizes. The paths to the beaches cut through scrubland covered with strongly scented wild oregano, a scattering of sage, and a profusion of thyme bushes that blaze bright purple in the spring. Tamarisk trees line the more frequented beaches, spreading their delicate fragrance when in flower and their welcome shade in the midday sun, while the invisible cicadas rend the air with their deafening chorus.

On a flag-stoned path winding its way up the Chora, out of a fine crack between two, tightly packed stone slabs, sprouts a single, bright orange, perfectly formed dandelion, its fine petals glistening in the sun. I pause to gaze at it and marvel at its defiant, unstunted growth in the absence of earth or space for its roots, revealing how even in the most unfavourable circumstances it is still possible to flourish.

I came here some years after my marriage broke up. I was also recently retired from my medical work, and my two daughters had grown up and were embarking on lives of their own. Here, where time stands still and space is wide open and free, I could find myself again. This island's elemental beauty and forthright simplicity, and the inner clarity and strength it inspires, may be what my mother was also searching for, and found, on another island in the Mediterranean Sea, a whole generation ago. She, though, was at the *start* of her adult life, and, as yet unknown to her, facing a relentless succession of harsh challenges that would stretch and test her to her limits.

The Balearic island of Mallorca

Käte, my mother, always recalled the Mallorcan village of Deià as the idyll of her life, her voice turning wistful and tender when she spoke of it, even from the opposite end of the earth, in New Zealand, the country which had offered us refuge, after Mexico, from the dangers we faced in a Europe ravaged by war. In the years leading up to all that, before the emergence of those complicated, menacing times, my mother had rented a village house with her close friend Seppl in Es Clot, on the edge of Deià, where it starts petering out on the way down through the steep meandering terraced olive groves, to the clinking of goat bells, to reach the small pebbled beach in the bay below.

Along with the friendly and welcoming locals, the two young women also became acquainted with a handful of young artists and poets recently settled in the small, untouched village of Deià of those years. Chief among them was Robert Graves, who – still shell shocked from the First World War – had found here the peace and quiet and simple living he sought. Spirited, dark-haired Käte, and Seppl with her porcelain good looks, enjoyed their new company and friends, and the sheer, unspoilt beauty of their surroundings, turning their stays in Deià into Käte's happiest and most carefree memories.

Apart from a rare reference to her early life, more a putting into words her thoughts than an intention to communicate them to me, she shared little about herself with me. In our fugitive life that consisted of one move after another demanding perpetual readjustment, she never had the leisure to relax with me, to share some carefree time together. Or tell me about herself.

It falls to me, then, to look for the pieces and fit them together; to try to reconstruct her life and make the connections that were missing between us during her lifetime – left in so many ways unfinished and unexplained. Many of the pieces and threads from our shared experiences, our spoken and unspoken interchanges, expressions of love and support or of strong disapproval and reprimand, were never followed through to an understanding or an explanation of what was happening around us. Or between us. They were left incomplete, a large question mark, a frustrating and troubled unknown, rather like our puzzlement as we strain to capture what has been left unworked and unresolved when we stand before an unfinished portrait...

I am attempting to see the world through her eyes, feel it through her senses, understand it through her intelligence. To retrace our path and find a way of bridging the increasing gap that developed between us over the years; to replace our apparent mismatch with a common understanding.

And make peace with her memory.

She left her photograph albums to my daughter Rebekah, believing I would not be interested in them. The photographs she took with her as she escaped, with me in one hand, and her suitcase with all our possessions in the other, across fields and roads, interminable journeys in dilapidated old buses, hidden under sagging beds in dingy hotel rooms, against a straw mattress in a communal hall full of refugees, and creaky bunks in shared ship cabins across the oceans.

I have borrowed the albums from Rebekah to study them.

My mother's photographs of Deià are lovingly arranged in two bijou-sized albums, their covers beautifully bound in raw linen and tied with a twisted silken cord. She has carefully placed a single photo in the middle of each page, separated and protected from each other by a fine translucent sheet embossed with a spider-web design.

Looking through them, they reveal a village of stone houses blending into the rocky landscape, all the way up the hill to the old church on the summit.

Street views display tall flowing palm trees, rows of umbrella pines, and an abundance of paddle cacti. In one photograph Seppl sits behind an ancient stone wall surrounded by a profusion of prickly pears, and in another a horse-drawn car-

The village of Deià, in the early 1930s

riage is driving past her as she walks along the coastal road in her straw hat with a basket slung across her shoulder. Details of house interiors reveal recesses cut into the white walls, bearing terracotta amphora jugs and local ceramic pots and plates.

Several views of the path that leads to the Cala in the bay below show people my mother would have known then. In one, the German artist Ulrich Leman, who formed part of the Otto Dix group as a young man, is painting in the landscape next to his easel. In another, the Scottish poet Norman Cameron squats on the beach nuzzling a small goat on his lap. A group of people, the men in straw hats and a boater, and the women in their pretty summer dresses with one sporting a flower in her hair, are grouped around a long table for what looks like a celebratory tea party on a garden terrace. Among them is a tall young man with thick, dark, untamed hair and the appearance of Robert Graves.

A view of the empty Cala from above has caught my mother Käte sitting on a large stone, suntanned and wind-blown, in deep conversation with a young man seated along-side, watching the waves wash up on the beach.

Käte and Seppl pose prettily together in their one-piece, wool-knit, bathing suits, or stretch out languidly on a rock taking the sun. Their small house on the edge of the village where Seppl sits on a stone-bench to one side of its arched, stone doorway, while, on its other side, a bunch of flowers and a bowl full of fruit rest on a rocky ledge on higher ground.

The side of the mountain is scattered with ancient olive trees, in black and white, gnarled and twisted into knotted, whirly shapes. These living sculptures date from medieval times

Festive group with Robert Graves and Ulrich Leman, in Deià

Käte amd friend in La Cala

when the Moors, then ruling Mallorca, turned the steep hillside into cultivated terraces. Their thousand-year-old stone walls still stand in the ochre landscape interspersed with the ash green of the olive trees and the darker green of the cypresses, palms and pines we see today.

On this Balearic island, my mother appears to have been at her happiest and freest, at one with the Mediterranean land and seascapes, she and Seppl relishing the warmth of the sun and of the local people, the olives, figs and bunches of flowers, long mountain walks, and indolent sunbathing in between their cool swims in the Cala.

Käte and Seppl took these breaks in Deià from their life in Barcelona where they had recently moved after their final, irre-

Seppl sitting outside the house in Es Clot

vocable parting from Germany, their native country, as the Nazi Party gained ground and Hitler took power. They had settled happily in Spain and become part of the bohemian, intellectual, left-wing circles that were forming in reaction to the unfolding events in Europe. Having completed their training in paediatric nursing in a children's hospital in Stuttgart, they were now working in Barcelona for well-to-do and often illustrious families who employed them for their expert care of their young children.

Among their many new acquaintances, they befriended a soulful, individualistic American of European origin, who had been living in Spain already for ten years, since the early twenties. Käte and Lou fell in love and started a relationship. She took him along on one of her visits to Italy to introduce him to her older sister, Lotte, who had settled in Florence with her two young children, when she too had moved out of their home in Germany, as the political situation and conditions became intolerable and the whole family dispersed.

At the height of their romance Käte and Lou decided to have a child, and they married in a simple civil ceremony to legitimise their liaison. However, differences and disagreements soon began to surface and they ended up living, by and large, their own separate lives – with Lou forever engaged in various diverse projects and travelling across country and continent, leading to prolonged and unpredictable absences.

And so it came to pass that my mother spent a large part of her pregnancy in the company of her close and loyal friend Seppl, back in her beloved Deià, where our own bond was taking root as she waited in joyous expectation for my birth.

La Floresta, inland near Barcelona

A large terrace at the back of Villa Pepita overlooks the fringes of the leafy village and the low-lying mountains beyond. As I gaze out from it, the sky is reddening over the woods and a symphony of dogs' barks from near and far fills the evening air. Tall, straight, stone pine trees, drooping cedars, dark leaved holm oaks and some graceful palms are silhouetted against the soft fiery horizon where the sun has just sunk behind the distant mountains, with Montserrat on the right. I sit in the gathering darkness, as my mother must have done – a lifetime ago, now – maybe in this very same spot, on this wide terrace, bordered by the stone balustrade so distinctive in the photos of my infancy, watching the same evening sky. I can see her in animated conversation with her German and Catalan friends, discussing the tense political situation and news of the day as the Spanish Civil War is about to break out, or maybe confiding their latest amorous and sexual encounters in the open and liberal milieu of their circle. By this hour I would have been tucked up in my cot in the tiny room at the top of the stairs in this, my first home, which up till now I knew only from the photographs my mother had so lovingly arranged in the album she made to record her new daughter's life.

I have been matching the photos with the house I am seeing again, after a lifetime's absence, and they have now suddenly acquired a three-dimensional character. They have turned from their longstanding, familiar, flat images into scenes that I can now walk around. I now know what lies on the other side, above, below or through that door or window in the photograph. The gate that leads from another balustrade-bordered terrace at the entrance of the house, to the small and now

Views of the house in La Floresta

paved street outside, is the same iron gate buttressed with two crossed rods that appears in many of the photos. The adjoining, twisted iron railing fence is also the same. Unchanged. What in the photos looks like a plain concrete floor inside the gate is now covered with large terracotta tiles, and two of the original four large terraces, which overlooked the wooded hills beyond, have been turned into a bedroom and a sunroom. But the house's tall, slim, distinct form, with its short-tiled roof sloping symmetrically from the top ridge to the gently uplifted edges either side – a characteristic of the houses of this period in La Floresta – identifies it as the house in my album's photos.

I was invited to come and stay for a few days by María, who currently lives in Villa Pepita, when I rediscovered it earlier this year during a visit to a friend in Barcelona. On the last day, before flying back to London, I made up my mind to take the train to La Floresta and look for the house. I brought a large copy of its photograph, which I had scanned from my album, and asked at the local bar – in which a group of men were standing around noisily drinking and exchanging stories – whether anyone recognised it. One of them pointed me in the direction of the older part of the village. After walking up a steep, interminably long flight of steps, I emerged onto a road with beautiful old homesteads half hidden in the luxuriant vegetation typical of La Floresta, with some bright yellow mimosa trees in its midst. A single man was at that moment walking towards me in the otherwise empty street. I approached him and showed him the photograph.

"Of course, I know this house, that is where my friend María lives," he exclaimed, interrupting his walk to take me to it. Gary turned out to be an Israeli, who had left his country and settled in La Floresta, and makes films and theatre on the theme of uprooted people searching for their origins. In an ensuing email, he declared that our meeting was no coincidence, adding, "when your heart leads you on a search and knows what it is you are looking for, reality 'bends itself towards you'..."

Yes... *Reality bends itself towards you.* Rather like the warping of space and time when they reach the speed of light. Or the transformation of matter into energy, or energy into matter, when they collide into each other.

Here, now, on my return, as I sit on this terrace, steeped in reflection, I can hear random phrases in my mother's warm voice wafting across the years. I can almost catch the faint echoes of her talk – deep in dialogue, in evenings just like this one – with her friends in the photographs.

Inside the house, at the top of the stairs and to the right of the landing, I found a small dark room. It is now used as a place to store brooms and buckets and various odds and ends. A tall window would look out onto the terrace below and the view beyond of the distant mountains, were it not permanently shuttered. It would also flood the room with the Catalan sunshine. But I prefer it like this, dark. I mentally empty the room of its present clutter and can see a cot in the far corner, the darkest part of the room, and in the cot, I – small and new to this world – lie in a deep sleep, oblivious to the anxieties and passions of the adults around me, their agreements and disagreements, the escalating war that will soon be upon us, the stress, the suffering, the treachery, the killing, none of which has affected me yet, or entered my still dormant, evolving consciousness. What bliss... If only I could recapture some part of it. I can hear my mother's tender voice, as she walks past the room, its door ajar, and glances towards the cot, "*Miri schläft*", half whispered to her friends so as not to disturb me.

It was here then, that I received my first and earliest impressions of the world around me: its colours, forms, smells, sounds, textures, and of the people in my vicinity, their faces, voices, expressions. My memories from that period, in my pre-verbal world, are of sensory experiences. I remember, from the mists of my recollections, the infinitely smooth velvet feel of my mother's earlobe I liked to stroke until I sank into sleep – the blurred division between myself and my mother gradually becoming sharper as I was growing distinct and becoming my own self. I can see the continuity between that small inquisitive creature who is emerging, learning to make sense of this world, to propel herself and stand and walk, the meaning of sounds

Käte with newborn Miriam in the corner of the front terrace

the adults made – in Spanish, German and Catalan, maybe English when my father is around – and so much else unfolding before her every day, and myself now, at an altogether different stage and moment in life. We are distinct entities, yet joined by a constant and consistent thread that runs through us across a lifetime of learning and experiences.

The other terrace, which is stepped onto through the front door of the house, overlooks the neighbour's red tiled roof, which slopes down towards its stone balustrade. This roof forms the background in many of the photos of the children of La Floresta, whom my mother befriended and kept an open house for. It was her passion for children that had led to her training as a paediatric nurse, before the Nazis' takeover prompted her departure from the country of her own childhood and youth.

I have been spending time also on this terrace that abuts the front of the house, sitting in the corner furthest from the iron gate to the street. For it is here where most of the photos in my mother's albums of those years were taken.

In front of me, on higher ground and to one side from the red tiled roof, two very tall stone pine trees next to a flat-roofed white house stand out against the skyline. As I face it from my corner on the terrace, that simple scene evokes a powerful sense of calm and déjà-vu, as though it has always been there and formed a part of me, instilled in the deepest hidden recess of my being. Many photos on this terrace are of me playing with the local children; others are of my mother and her visiting friends, or of my father with me or on his own, sitting in this very same corner where the stone balustrade meets the front wall of the house.

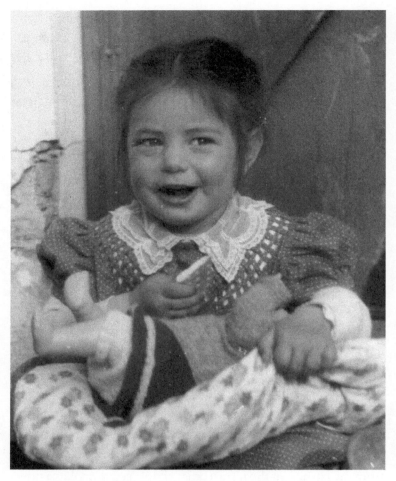

Miriam's second birthday, playing with her new toys inside the iron gate

I remember Lali. She and I play together in the photos, fully absorbed with our dolls in their toy prams, just inside the iron gate. The date in my mother's handwriting, on that page of the album, is my second birthday.

In another photograph, we are reclining under two parasols, side by side, in the bright sunshine.

Agustí Duran i Sanpere was Lali's father and a close friend of my mother. He was a revered historian and the curator of the Catalonian historical archives in Barcelona, who would not so much take sides in the intense political debates of the day as assiduously protect Catalonia's historical art treasures from the widespread destruction that would take place between the various warring factions. When, twenty-five years later, we returned to Europe and Barcelona from New Zealand, my mother sought him out and they celebrated their reunion sitting quietly together, lost in conversation, watching the ancient Catalan dance of *Las Sardanas* in Plaza Cataluña, as I imagine they would have done in those earlier times.

My mother sits with Seppl poised across her lap, both of them listening attentively to *Avis* Campalans, his wife on the

Käte, Seppl, Avis Campalans and friends in the corner of the front terrace

bench next to him and a group of friends perched on the balustrade behind them, as Campalans – wearing a pince-nez and sporting a moustache and a goatee, a handkerchief peeping out of his suit's top pocket, and a cigar gripped between his fingers – holds the rapt attention of the whole group with his words.

They too are in this corner of the terrace where I am sitting now, this warm evening, resurrecting ghosts from the past... *Avis*, I find out, is Catalan for grandparents: the elderly Campalans couple must have been Seppl's in-laws, the parents of Rafael Campalans i Puig.

Rafael Campalans was a physicist, university professor, writer and much admired Catalan socialist politician who had tried to mend the inexorable sectarian political infighting going on in Catalonia and the Spanish Republic at the time. His first wife had died in childbirth, leaving him a widower with two children. He first met Seppl and my mother, the two of them dressed in Mexican *charro* outfits with narrow trousers and big sombreros, at a fancy-dress party in Barcelona. He developed a close friendship with the two women and spent many times in their company, finally proposing to Seppl. It was a happy but tragically short marriage. Barely a year later, as they were preparing for a large festive reception and dinner for a group of friends in Rafael's beach house in Torredembarra, having just finished decorating it with some colourful lampions for the occasion, he decided to take a short, pre-lunch swim with Seppl and his two children, and a sudden squall and swell in the sea seems to have dashed him against the rocks. He could not be saved.

My mother was in New York at the time, where a couple

had taken her on their travels to tend to their child, but on hearing the sad news from Seppl she came back to comfort her and be at her side in Barcelona. Rafael's tragic death was reported in the Catalan newspapers, dated "9 September, 1933". The photo with *Avis* Campalans on this terrace in Villa Pepita was taken two years later. I was not yet born.

My father also appears in photographs in this same corner of the terrace. He stands here, leaning back against the balustrade, in an open shirt and jacket, his dark hair tousled back, a cigarette in his mouth, staring thoughtfully and intently into the camera. In another photo, I am sitting astride his shoulders with Seppl behind him holding me firmly sandwiched between the two of them – there I am, wedged between my mother's two, quite different, loves. Though my father was clearly not living with us, he must have rented Villa Pepita. I have a nebulous but intense memory of his visits, of his lifting me high in the air and burying his face and blowing raspberries into my tummy and kissing the soles of my feet, making me giggle with pleasure and rejoice in my small chubby feet.

My mother never knew where Lou, my father, was. Or where he went or when he would return or what he was doing between his visits.

From some notes he wrote about his life and passed on to me in his later years, I now know that he earned his living running a business of skins and leather which he supervised personally – he writes that his fingertips bled from his constant testing for the quality of the various samples he sent in bulk to countries abroad – and by which he amassed a considerable fortune. He refers to meetings back and forth with a large and diverse network of friends and acquaintances, including writers, artists and intellectuals, some surely dating from his contacts and activities in the north of Spain, near the French border, some fifteen years earlier during the First World War, when he had been recruited by the Americans into counterintelligence. Now he was participating in the Spanish war by putting out radio bulletins in English, meeting overseas journalists, reporting his own first-hand, on the ground, observations, and ferrying them around in his Ford convertible. Besides getting into various scrapes, from which he always seemed to emerge unscathed. He persuaded one American newspaper man that, contrary to the mistaken American perspective of the Spanish populace fighting Franco as being predominantly communist, it was actually largely made up of the anarcho-syndicalist movement. He pointed out to the journalist that this was a legitimate party represented in the government, and that he had seen its system successfully at work, centred on team-work and communal responsibility. He drew the American correspondent's attention to its efficacy, as well, in urban Barcelona, where public institutions such as the electricity service, the post office, and the banks, were also being run under this scheme. The communists, on the other hand, made up only a small fraction of the population, though Stalin's backing had given them disproportionate power. Back in New York, the journalist was fired by his newspaper upon publishing his article, based on my father's observations.

In his notes, my father also describes a trip on a bitterly cold winter's night from Madrid to Barcelona. His hands were frozen and he had a terrible pain in the back of his neck. He downed a bottle of Cognac, he writes, in order to face the long drive which crossed the front line of the, by now, advanced fighting at several points. He was giving a lift to a woman and her daughter who were trying to reach Valencia. He set off in his hoodless car, the night was dark and moonless, the road a ribbon of ice all the way, and in parts so narrow that he had to mount the adjoining field to let the occasional oncoming vehicle pass. And all that, with no headlights... He managed to drop his two passengers in Valencia and reach Barcelona in one piece.

He had formed a deep attachment to Spain, where he felt at one with the people and the country in which he had lived for more than a decade by then, and he was eager to help in the war effort against Franco and his supporters. Not only were they well armed, and served additionally by a large contingent of Moroccan troops, but they also had backing from Hitler's, Mussolini's, and Salazar's disciplined and well-stocked armies. The Republic, on the other hand, was ill prepared and ill equipped, and Stalin's assistance fitful and counterproductive, as he became increasingly preoccupied with wiping out the anarchists and dissident communists.

In my father's resolve to persuade the United States of the need for intervention and military assistance to the Republican side, he decided to make a documentary film. He set about producing it with the use of many reels of film he acquired from reporters in the battlefield, as well as from newsreels, documentaries and other sources. He spent many long hours editing this vast material and preparing a commentary for it, with the objective of telling the story of Spain's true position as he saw it. He finally produced two films, *Fury Over Spain*, followed by *The Will of a People*, which was the more extensively edited and complete. They were screened in New York, where he travelled each time for the occasion. *The Will of a People* was shown in February 1939, in the Belmont Cinema on Broadway; it was received with interest and, he claims, great emotion, and was reviewed across the papers from *The New York Times* to *The Daily Worker*. Even so, the war by then was already coming to an end, and the Republic defeated.

I recently came across a Catalan film historian, Pau Martinez Muñoz, who has studied my father's films in depth. We found we had much to talk about: she wanted to hear all I knew about my father and I was interested in her research into his films. She suggested meeting, and invited me to stay with her at her charming, small apartment in Poble Sec, in Barcelona. From her back balcony covered with pot plants, I looked out into an inner court encircled with apartment buildings like her own, with the blue Mediterranean sea stretching to the horizon beyond them, while from a front balcony the dazzling domes of the seventeenth-century castle and fortress, in the nearby park of Montjuïc, stood out against the Catalan skyline. The castle has seen much history, and is known, among other things, as the infamous site of torture and executions during the civil war.

Pau has researched and become a leading authority on the anarchist cinema that was filmed and produced during the Spanish Civil War.

"Your father's documentaries, which he made from film material he collected and edited during the Spanish Civil War, are the only ones to have survived in their entirety, apart from one other film. All the rest – and there were a great many – were destroyed in a fire of the building where they were stored during Franco's dictatorship," she told me. She spoke at length about their important contribution as witness to the events at the time, and we sat and watched her copies of them.

These, then, would appear to be some of my father's adventures and enterprises while my mother and I spent our time in la Floresta. And, once in a while, when he happened to be in Barcelona during a gap from his travels and commitments, he would turn up at Villa Pepita and lift me up and carry me on his shoulders and tickle my feet or lie, relaxed, on this terrace, a few feet from where I am sitting now, playing with what look like chess pieces on the floor, me leaning contentedly against him.

Lou with Miriam on the front terrace, La Floresta

I am coming to the end of my stay at Villa Pepita in La Floresta. María – who so generously suggested I come and stay while she is away on holiday, that day when Gary brought me here and introduced me to her and told her of my connection with the house – will soon be back. I have been watering her pot plants lined along the foot of the balustrade in the front terrace and on the steps leading from it to the garden below, and I am now relaxing and reminiscing again at the end of the day.

Evening is falling, and the sky is blushing a deep red through the foliage behind the house where the ground, with its ancient trees and rich undergrowth, drops steeply to the street below. Villa Pepita can be entered from the small street that runs alongside the house above, Carrer del Deposit, or by climbing up to it along a twisting path through the trees from the Major de la Floresta below. The calm that envelops me as I sit in this corner of the terrace near the main door into the house, the rural silence and the softly diminishing evening light, gives me a sense of profound peace as I travel through time − no, time has stopped and stands still, past and present merged into one: I am here as I am now and as I was then, both at one and the same time. I have broken through the time barrier and am floating freely in this removed timeless dimension. I am lying in the cot next to my mother who sits here with her friends. I have been brought here fresh from the clinic in Barcelona, and am sleeping soundly yet also taking in − at some deep, dark, instinctive level − these surroundings. The two pines and the white house above will soon make their way into my emerging consciousness and become engrained into my being. The front door of the house is always open and people move freely back and forth between this terrace and the main room inside. Now I can hear my mother's voice calling out something in German as she comes out of the house to join her friends on the terrace. I can sense their presence here. They are visiting, maybe staying a few days; I, the small newcomer, the centre of attention that forms part of their camaraderie and talk and discussion on this terrace. It has become a place of reunion for these German friends who are here on an ideological quest following their country's Nazi takeover, and now facing Spain's convulsive crackdown as the Republic threatens to disintegrate under attack from Franco's armies and supporters. They discuss endlessly what is the right thing to do without ever finding a solution. One German communist friend is always accompanied by his large, brown, friendly Labrador. I don't remember the man's name but the dog's was Trompi. Catalan friends from Barcelona and La Floresta also form part of the scene, as well as the local children who always feel welcome and come to hold the new baby and take her for walks and play. Here, in the peace of La Floresta, there is a general sense of freedom, trust and community spirit in its thickly wooded, mountainous ambience.

Yet elsewhere in Spain the forces are gathering and mounting. The streets in the centre of Barcelona are even now already overrun with restless protesting crowds ready to sacrifice all for their rights, freedom and ideologies as they prepare for the bloody confrontation about to break out. Huge banners hang from balconies, posters blare out their parties' messages, and notices reporting the latest news on the rapidly changing situation are thronged by people who are eagerly studying them. The largest popular party here in Catalonia is the anarcho-syndicalist movement. It is allied to the Unified Marxist Workers Party, or POUM, made up of the dissident communists opposed to Stalin, which George Orwell joined. The smaller, hard-core, Stalinist communists form the PSUC, which has a strong representation in the Catalan government, contingent to Stalin's military assistance. Hubert von Ranke heads its foreign

Hubert and Seppl on the back terrace, La Floresta

section and will soon serve in the government's department for intelligence, *Grupo de Información del Estado*, under the command of Stalin's proficient, if ominous, NKVD directives.

Photos of Seppl on the back terrace of Villa Pepita, where it hangs over the steep drop towards the road below, Major de la Floresta, and looks out onto the wooded hills beyond, show her sitting on the balustrade with Hubert von Ranke, to whom she has now become romantically attached.

In one, Hubert stands alone leaning into the corner of the balustrade: a slim, sinewy young man, hair smoothed back from his receding hairline, his penetrating look from his lowered face, bold, lean and steely.

Hubert came from a German aristocratic family, and was a

first cousin of Robert Graves, who was also known as Robert von Ranke Graves – though he dropped the 'von Ranke' with its distasteful German association to him, while still maintaining a warm and cordial relation with his cousin. He was a descendant of the historian Leopold von Ranke, who is remembered for his introduction of the use of original sources in history, in search of the facts, "to show what actually hap-

Hubert von Ranke, La Floresta

pened". To glean the truth – in contradiction to the inextricable tangled trail of manipulation and misinformation that characterises, and will long follow, this war. Hubert had joined the Communist Party in Germany, as my mother and Seppl and many of their German friends had done, in the face of the rising tide of National Socialism and the ideological wars of the time – though Hubert's driven zeal and dedication had led to his joining the party's militant faction.

Meanwhile, my mother would leave me in the care of her friends in La Floresta and go into Barcelona where she worked in the post office, combing through and censoring German mail. She also attended meetings of the Communist Party where she mixed with and met many members who would play prominent roles. One, Ramon Mercader, whom she remembered as an unremarkable, quiet young man who mostly kept to himself, would be Trotsky's assassin in Mexico a few years hence. She would sit and listen to the instructions from Moscow and express her disagreement and argue against them. But orders are to be carried out, you don't ask questions, she was sternly reprimanded. The initial promise of the Party, during her years in Berlin, when she had watched the Nazification of Germany before Stalin's purges started or became known, was now wearing thin. She became increasingly disillusioned and perturbed by what she was witnessing and finally left the Party. Like so many others.

My mother was in La Floresta, with me just six weeks old, when she received the news of the death of her mother, Clara, in her hometown, Chemnitz, in Germany. Clara had been ill for some time, but my mother was unable to visit her after her last and final trip to Germany, in 1933, when Hitler became

Chancellor and effectively took power. Having left Germany and with her citizenship revoked, she was now stateless with all its attendant complications and predicaments.

She once described to my, at the time, still very young daughter how the day she received the news of her mother Clara's death she retired into her room and wept for a week... Was it the upstairs, front bedroom, with the two tall windows – three in my mother's time, the middle one has been blocked up – that look down onto this terrace, with its inner door across the landing from my tiny room? I can see her stretched across her bed in the light spacious room, maybe she has drawn the curtains to mourn quietly in the dark, her slender, shapely body crumpled with grief, sobbing fitfully and softly to herself. She would be remembering her mother's smiling kindly face from her childhood, mixed with her more recent memories of Clara pained and disillusioned in the face of the changing world around her, and her beloved daughter Käte's revolutionary conduct and ideas – so opposed to everything she herself had stood for and taught her. The neat, conservative, orderly way of life she had been used to, and brought her children up to. My mother would be thinking of her father too, pining for his loss by himself, all his four children having left Germany. He would be alone, from now on, in the large, family garden flat which had not so long ago been full of their chatter, cheer and lively activity.

She must have been at the height of a mother's bliss and elation at her new maternal role with her recently born child – a brand new life which had come into hers and required her full attention and love and protection, a nucleus of hope and joy amid all the sinister confusion and uncertainty all around her –

when she was plunged into this deep new sorrow as she faced her final parting from her mother who had borne and cherished her, and whom she would never see again. All this, she would have been trying to digest and understand, as she found herself in this new country, irretrievably cut off from the old, trying to come to terms with her bereavement. She must have felt, at this moment, very alone... Such a stark contrast from her recent past, when her life had been so full and happy, with herself in control of it, working with children she cared for, travelling widely, forming rich friendships and attracting devoted lovers. She especially remembered from her Berlin years the exciting, compelling actor, Alexander Granach, who had been very enamoured of her. Life back then had seemed to hold so much promise; now she felt forlorn and forgotten. She had made new friends here, and had grown closer to her older ones, but they were tied up with their own lives. Even Seppl was being drawn away now by her new relationship with Hubert. And she could not count on Lou who came and went without warning or explanation. In her photo album covering the time when she would have met him and first knew him, there is a single photograph of my father in warm, pensive mood – he looks like a poet in this one – yet from the rest of that page and the ones before and after it, the photos have been torn out and scratched down to the messy leftover bits that the glue wouldn't give up, in contrast to the rest of the album which has been put together with so much care.

The loss then of her mother, and her severance from her native home and close-knit family, must have made her suddenly feel out on her own, in this big, wide, fickle world. She must have been going through a welter of emotions as she tried to deal with this news, having just given birth and on the verge of war, all at once, in this, her newly adopted country.

In this house, Villa Pepita, in La Floresta, to which I have returned in search of my beginnings and the world I came into, I retrieved my mother and my father and the people who passed through it during those momentous days, and I heard their voices echoing across the years so close I could all but feel their breaths in their animated exchanges of their passionate ideologies, their forming and breaking friendships, their great joys and deep disillusions. This piece of ground and space that they and I stood in and occupied, where these events were played out, *bent itself* to merge with the two points in time. Two periods, so many years and tears apart, coalesced into one consciousness.

London and Paris Palette

London, by the River Thames

Glinting metallic crimson and russet reflections ripple and flicker across the watery expanse of the river. On the facing bank, the roofs of the Chelsea Harbour buildings and the Lots Road power station, with its two piercingly tall chimneys, are silhouetted against a narrow strip of clear sky glowing scarlet and liquid gold beneath the thick leaden blanket of cloud that looms over London, horizon to horizon.

J.M.W. Turner, in his Chelsea years, is said to have been rowed by his servant, every day, across this section of the Thames, to paint the river scene from the vestry window of the small church, far below me, next to my building. St Mary's is an austere, dark brick, rectangular building, with a high pointed clock tower and steeple, built in the eighteenth century on the site of its predecessor, thought to date from Saxon times. In this church too, William Blake was married, and other renowned historical characters rest their bones in ancient tombs scattered about its yard. From my position I also look down on four large residential barges moored to the river wall that borders St Mary's churchyard.

I moved a few years ago to this, my new London home, on the eighth floor of an apartment building that forms part of a growing group of developments massing along the banks of the Thames, from Putney upriver all the way to the City, Canary Wharf and beyond, on its course to the estuary. They have radically changed the face of the old, in many parts still

Dickensian, London that I found when I first arrived in this country. From where I sit, a different Turneresque sunset lights up the skies and river that stretch before me every evening.

From this corner in my living room I can see joggers and cyclists, women pushing prams, and men walking their dogs along the riverside path. And birds. Seagulls, singly or in flocks, wave, coast and swoop over the river, and, at certain times of the year, starlings appear in great numbers and fly in formation displaying their astonishing aerobatics. In the spring, Canadian geese share the large patch of green lawn, at the foot of the building, with the picnickers and sunbathers who congregate there when the sun comes out, or they drift with the tide in the murky water followed by their goslings. And, every now and then, two majestic white swans make their appearance gliding close to the riverbank, one always lagging a good distance behind the other.

I sit before my square coffee table with some art books piled on one corner: Georgiana Colvile's *Scandaleusement d'Elles* on the women surrealist artists in the twentieth century, Matisse's *JAZZ* book with his primary colour cut-outs and hand-written reflections, and the recently published edition of Kortokraks artworks. The small oak table fits in the corner of the L-shaped, natural linen sofa that occupies this end of the room, and matches the oak bookshelf that stretches across the inner wall of the living room and houses my books, from floor to ceiling. In its narrower sections, the bookshelf displays three handsome photographs of my grandsons, some hand-painted Berber ceramics, two intricately fashioned Chinese mari-onettes, a collection of pre-Columbian clay figurines, and other tokens and artefacts from past travels. Across the room is the dining-table with a Mexican runner and a bowl full of fruit. A few paintings hang on the walls, and a green jungle of plants cluster in the centre of the river view. These make up my living space here.

I moved to this apartment when I no longer needed the space of my previous home, in Islington, north of the river – a terraced Georgian house facing an avenue of tall linden trees and the Regent's Canal beyond. The extensive ground floor and basement through-rooms had been turned into the studios used by my husband, Kortokraks, and were crammed with his art works. At one time he ran a school in the ground floor studio, every Sunday, teaching a handful of people who wished to develop further their painting skills. The students were a varied and dedicated group spread across all ages and national-ities, the artistic director of the London Contemporary Dance Company, Robert Cohan, being one of his most committed and enthusiastic. The studio would become suffused with a magic ambience of transported creativity under Kortokraks' inspirational teaching, marred here and there by incomprehen-sible angry remonstrations from the temperamental teacher. He also held exhibitions of his works on the two floors, which were attended by a wide and appreciative following.

I, on the other hand, made my daily journey to the Royal London and Newham General Hospitals, in London's East End, where I spent my days in the operating theatre, giving anaesthetics and supervising and teaching doctors in training, engaging in research, and lecturing nurses, medical students and postgraduates. My special interest in obstetric anaesthesia turned it into my sub-specialty. I enjoyed the challenge of assisting expectant mothers with the births of their infants and relieving their pain, whether on their request to make them more comfortable or through clinical necessity in a difficult labour, right across a wide spectrum of medical situations and emergencies, to an awake, painless, caesarean section when complications demanded intervention. This facilitated early bonding between mother and new-born infant, and the celebration of the baby's arrival by both parents, even in the face of grave clinical adversity. Merging the highly skilled with the humane.

My life then was divided between the rigorous demands of my hospital work, Kortokraks, and our two growing daughters, not necessarily always in that order.

In the heart of cosmopolitan Islington, the busy and colourful Chapel market offered endless stands of fresh fruit and vegetables, flowers and plants, household goods, all kinds of clothing and various sundry trinkets. Cafés and restaurants from every corner of the world lined the high street, and, round the corner from the house in Duncan Terrace, the bustling antique market, Camden Passage, drew connoisseurs and tourists from near and far, while Regent's Canal could be glimpsed through our windows when the linden trees lost their foliage in winter. In later years, I would take a walk with my small new grandson along the banks of the canal and we would observe the life around the moored narrowboats, enjoy the view of the wide basin and lock further on, and stop to feed and watch the ducks and coots cruising and zigzagging along their course, rippling the water and breaking up the reflections.

But that is all past now. And the time came to move on.

I was facing four storeys of the family's possessions and baggage accumulated over a lifetime – clothes, books, work files, the huge number of paintings and rest of my husband's artwork which he had left behind, my daughters' outgrown belongings which had also been entrusted to me for their storage, and some of my mother's household and other goods that she had taken with her from the various homes and countries she had lived in, whether through enforced migration or her choice, in later years, driven by her unsettled life.

It had been there, in my Duncan Terrace home, that we had celebrated her last birthday, her cancer already advanced. We invited all her friends and prepared a buffet of tasty finger-food and choux cream puffs, which my daughters lovingly helped to prepare for the occasion – though she only managed tiny nibbles, her appetite already gone by then. She cut a frail and delicate figure, sunk in the large armchair in her best chiffon dress, drawing on what energy she could muster to talk every now and then with her friends.

She died a few months later.

And now I was preparing to move out from that house, trying to digest my many conflicting memories as I went through the accumulated hoard of household and family belongings spanning three generations and an estranged husband. What to keep and what to dispose of, from more recent acquisitions as well as much stuff that had lain forgotten and stored away over the years.

I had lived in the Duncan Terrace house for twenty-four years. Before that, my life had been on the move, sometimes more and others less, all the way back from my beginnings in La Floresta. A variety of temporary basic rooms in France as my mother and I moved from place to place, keeping a step ahead of the Vichy French police and invading Germans, our frugal years in Mexico, also marked by frequent changes of rented accommodation, and then New Zealand where we first found ourselves crammed in my aunt's front room, followed by our own lodgings while I attended high school, and then onto a variety of students' digs and hospital accommodation during my medical studies. After qualifying and completing my hospital training, the pattern continued back in Europe and a brief spell in the Middle East. During all those moves I had not had a definitive, long-term home. Here, in this leafy corner of London's Islington, I had found a stable residence. The time had come to dismantle it and pick through my gathered possessions, mementos and memories, and decide what to keep, what to give away, what to throw out.

I rediscovered old schoolbooks from my Mexican childhood, medical lecture notes from my New Zealand university years, pretty dresses I had worn in my youth and more formal suits from my work days, my daughters' first knitted baby garments, their toys and their schoolbooks. They all vividly brought back the past. They were also tangible proofs of my memories: to see some of these things for the last time before throwing them into the bin bag was like watching a small part of me die. Closing a coffin lid on them. Yet it was also cutting off dead wood and making space for new shoots, ideas and life.

My earliest recollection of loss came back to me then. We had already made many moves and left much behind before that occasion, but I was either too young to understand the finality of what we didn't take with us, or too busy taking in and adapting to my new surroundings every time, to give it much significance. Of this particular loss, though, I always retained a startlingly clear memory. We had left Europe behind in the grip of the Second World War, and had just arrived on a large ship packed with refugees, my mother and myself, aged five, across the Atlantic Ocean to the Mexican port of Veracruz. My mother was carrying by hand the suitcase and small trunk that contained all our worldly possessions at the time, as we walked along the road to catch the bus to Mexico city, when I suddenly realised I had left my pillow in the small, basic hotel room where we had spent our first night in our new country. That flat, white, embroidered, semi-circular pillow, with a pretty flounce around its curved edge, was the only familiar object I still had from the start of my life in La Floresta, on which I looked forward to laying my head and sleeping every night. I remember crying at my loss of that pillow as though my right hand had been cut off...

Leaving behind and letting go of things from the past is rather like that, like chipping off a part of oneself. Yet it also makes room for the new, a liberation from props, a breaking free that allows renewal. Those things that matter are finally kept in our memories and in our hearts.

As I emptied the house in Duncan Terrace, with the date of my move drawing closer, I also came across old letters from Kortokraks: some tender and plaintive, others obscure, many truculent and angry. A file with my bank statements: proof of my dogged persistence over the years to provide for him and the family against whatever odds, and its only physical record – and I lamented that my experiences should have led me to think of it in this way. The large collection of art works that he had left behind when we separated and he moved out, which filled a large part of the studio, were packed into a container for long-term storage. Among the paintings – portraits, landscapes, historical and political mixed-media collages and pow-erful statements – there was also an unfinished portrait of me: one eye a green splodge waiting for the next brushstroke, the other alive enough already...

When I started my new life in this apartment, where the river view replaced the avenue of linden trees in Duncan Terrace, I left the walls white and empty in my attempt to clear the clutter of my life from my head. There was something soothing and calming about being surrounded by clean white walls and the view of the smooth flat surface of the river and not much else. Eventually, when I had sufficiently untangled my thoughts and emotions, I put up some watery Venice scenes on my walls – Kortokraks's economically achieved strokes, dabs, lines and smudges on the thick hand-made paper catching the movement of the water and bobbing gondolas against the Venetian skyline, complementing the Thames view out of my window.

It has been a long journey from our straw mattress on the floor of a communal hall in Casablanca, shared with a shipload of refugees on course from Marseilles to Veracruz in 1941, all the way to my home in this apartment block. I am an extension of that little girl, along with everything I have experienced and learnt since then and am still exploring and will never finish fathoming out – much as the unfinished portrait also express-es.

My mother's trunk and suitcase, with everything we were taking from the Old World to the New, stood on the narrow strip of floor between our mattress and the next, which homed another family, in the long row of mattresses lying side by side in that vast hall in Casablanca. The photograph albums must have been in the trunk. It suddenly dawns on me, for the first time, that my mother must have taken them with her in our every move in France, on some occasions with little warning as the advancing Germans entered the area where we were sheltering and hiding from them, necessitating a quick getaway with her small daughter and whatever she could take with her.

Other things were replaceable, but the photos were important. Those captured, frozen moments of her early life events and activities, of her close family and stable home from her childhood, her devoted work with the children she had minded, her many friends and considerable travels, were all witness to the promise of her youth, before the Spanish and World wars crushed everything and left her clinging on to survive with her young child. The photos were her aide-mémoire to those happier, adventurous, more carefree times. They were her past, a tangible, visible proof of an earlier, still unfractured identity.

The river sparkles below me as I sit here with my mother's albums spread around me. They range in size, from the two miniature ones that she dedicated to her Deià photographs, to various medium sized, through to large. Each has been carefully bound with a different linen fabric in subtle, natural, earthy colours which have been woven into the linen, or stamped on it in a striped, checked or abstract design.

I pick one up in which she mounted her photos of a child she was looking after in England. On one of the first pages she wrote, "*Oliver Penrose, März - Dezember 1930*". She had not yet moved to Barcelona, and was still able to visit her family and friends in Germany. My mother had always referred to the children who had been in her charge during those years with great fondness, and Oliver appeared to have occupied pride of place in her affections. In the album dedicated to her time with him, she faithfully records his age in months, as the pages are turned and he grows older, and the places where the photos were taken, her language a mix of English and German: I can see her switching over to English from her mother tongue around this time. A faded sepia photograph shows Oliver's parents, Lionel and Margaret Penrose, standing at the door of a large house with a thatched roof, with "Green Tye Cottage" neatly written in her German Gothic handwriting underneath.

Others are labelled in Wales, where she had gone with the family to a country house. She saw much of southern Britain, from World's End to the West Country, to Hertfordshire and

Lionel and Margaret Penrose at Green Tye Cottage

to Oxford, from where she kept sharply defined, black and white postcards of many of the colleges. Over the page is another sepia photograph of a large Tudoresque residence, with many conical and heptagonal turrets covered in Virginia and floral creepers, and a water lily pond in a secluded corner of its extensive grounds, under which she has written, "Oxhey Grange, near Watford". This appears to be the Penrose family home where Lionel had grown up in his parents' artistic, Quaker household.

Seppl had preceded my mother at the Penroses, and both women had developed a close work friendship with the family. My mother lived with them while she looked after Oliver in his first year, and returned a year later when his brother Roger was born. She spoke of their father Lionel with admiration: he was a doctor, scientist, mathematician and renowned geneticist, while Oliver would become a mathematician and Roger a philosopher. Lionel's brother, Roland Penrose, was more artistically inclined and went to Paris, where he became closely involved with the Surrealists and their new evolving ideas and experimentation. He became an active participant of their group and lively art scene.

Around the same time, and several years before he was to meet my mother, Lou often travelled to Paris where he became acquainted with various individuals in the same circle of free thinking, innovative artists and intellectuals. He also spent time in London where he mixed with and befriended people whose principles and outlook he shared and actively supported, with whom he would keep in touch over the years – the British anarchist publisher Vernon Richards, and the Labour politician Jenny Lee, amongst them. In these circles he also came to know Roland Penrose, who – years later, when the Spanish Civil War broke out – would organise a touring exhibition in Britain of Picasso's painting of *Guernica*, to raise awareness and funds for the Spanish Republicans against Franco and his

Fascist allies Hitler and Mussolini, as my father attempted with his films in the U.S.

My mother and father, along with every other thinking person of those times, became deeply involved and caught up in the widespread upheaval from the emerging, and opposing, revolutionary ideologies. These new concepts against the old established bourgeois orders were turning one persuasion against the other, leading to disagreements, conflicts, and worse, even within the same group. Artists, poets and writers were drawn into the struggle for justice and freedom, and became deeply engaged in exploring radically new ways and founding new movements to express the convulsive changes they were living through. Art, ideology and politics became closely entwined, and one medium embodied the other.

The Paris my father would have known has been described as a euphoric and feverish explosion bent on renewing mankind following the First World War. This was a time in which Albert Einstein was stretching the boundaries of the known physical world and Sigmund Freud of the mysterious world of dreams and the subconscious, following closely on Karl Marx's vision of a new social order and economy.

Many of these artists, thinkers and literary figures had embarked on their new art forms, debates and exchanges at the turn of the century in a remarkable construction off a square in Montmartre. This old, ramshackle, wooden complex of workshops and living quarters, once connected by a maze of dark and dingy corridors and stairways, chronicled as reeking of mildew and cat piss, became known as "Le Bateau Lavoir", for its resemblance to the laundry barges in the River Seine. Its struggling artistic community lived and worked in what has been described as a tangled mass of glass panels and wooden log beams that creaked and swayed in the wind. The whole building was served by a single communal tap of cold water and a primitive hole-in-the-ground lavatory at the bottom landing of the lower floors, which emerged into another street round the corner below.

Le Bateau Lavoir attracted young, impecunious Spanish and Italian artists freshly arrived in Paris, including the nine-teen-year-old Pablo Picasso, Juan Gris and Amedeo Modigliani. It was here that Picasso and Braque experimented with the new art form of Cubism – exploring the idea of breaking up objects into their various three dimensional parts and restructuring them on the canvas to represent the whole – which would inspire and influence much of what followed. Le Bateau Lavoir became the lively, much frequented, popular meeting point for their friends and fellow artists, Matisse, Utrillo, Dufy, Renoir, Gauguin and many others, and also poets, writers,

Le Bateau Lavoir, in the early 1900s

theatre and dance personalities, art and literary patrons and benefactors, and the eminent art dealers of the day – not to forget girlfriends, models, lovers and other sundry visitors.

The original Bateau Lavoir's wooden buildings were largely destroyed by fire in 1970, but it has since been reconstructed, along with a small gallery at one end of the square, which has been renamed Place Émile Goudeau.

Today, when I visit Paris, I stay with my friend Nicole Milhaud at her Bateau Lavoir studio, the sole surviving area of the original structure, round the corner from the enchanting, leafy, Place Émile Goudeau, half-way up to the Sacré-Coeur Basilica at the top of Montmartre. Long, vertical, overlapping slats of glass that stretch across the full width of the studio's façade are topped by another similar inclined tier that forms the roof. At the base of the glass frontage, Nicole's pot plants provide a dripping curtain of green foliage and a burst of bright colours.

Nicole is a petite, ebullient, indefatigable woman with a mass of reddish hair piled on top of her head and olive green eyes heavily rimmed with kohl. When her face breaks into a smile, all her joy, warmth and generosity towards humankind light up her intense eyes. She recently retired from her law practice with her office in Montmartre, on the edge of Pigalle, Paris' red-light district, a few minutes' walk from her studio. She was known for taking on all the disadvantaged and poverty-stricken cases in Paris that nobody else would defend. I remember fetching her from her office, at the end of her day's work, on a visit to her some years ago. We walked back to her studio through the narrow streets where the mixed local population mingles with the tourists and, as night falls, prosti-

Nicole Milhaud's studio

tutes and transvestites hang around chatting and waiting for clients. Nicole would stop, kiss them on both cheeks and exchange lengthy animated conversations with every one of them before moving on.

It was plain to see how much everybody in the *quartier* loves Nicole.

When I first met her, she was married to Daniel Milhaud, who had taught with Kortokraks at the international art school that ran during Salzburg's music festival season, and was headed at the time by Oscar Kokoschka. Daniel was the son of Madelaine and Darius Milhaud, the French composer, whom Kortokraks also came to know and befriend.

Inside Nicole's studio, the main room is full of paintings and sculptures by her second, Dutch husband, Theys Willemse, wooden shelves crammed with a collection of books and other objects, and a large round dining table with various reminders on it and around the room from her busy life. A fireplace has a mantelpiece above it full of her favourite objects, including old family photographs, a carved wooden sandal Theys brought back from Korea, a brass Menorah from Nicole's Polish-Ashkenazi background at one end, and at the other a Mexican terracotta Tree of Life candelabra, glazed purple, pink, blue and green, with a little bird in the middle. Behind the room are a tiny crowded kitchen and bathroom, which look out onto the other studios, on the lower ground at the back, that make up today's reconstructed complex of Le Bateau Lavoir.

Darius Milhaud also became part of that group of artists and intellectuals drawn together by the ferment of ideas swirling around, at that critical crossroads of new perspectives. A breaking away and radical rethink of the old traditional values, to experiment and launch into revolutionary new forms, creating novel ways of deciphering and seeing the world in the aftermath of Marx and Freud and other thinkers and figures of the late nineteenth and early twentieth centuries. Milhaud shook up the more traditional European concepts in music composition as he wove American jazz and Latin American rhythms into the fabric of his avant-garde, bewitching musical creations. He formed part of Les Six, and created music for the theatre and the Ballets Rousses in collaboration with Diaghilev, Cocteau and Picasso. Kortokraks painted a portrait of him, when he met him in his later years, which was acquisitioned by Mills College, in Oakland, California, where Milhaud taught for many years.

As you enter Nicole's studio from the street, a wooden staircase leads from the front of the main all-purpose room to the tiny bedroom, where I stay when I am in Paris, tucked under the sloping, glass-slatted roof, through which I look out onto the tall trees and ivy clad houses of Montmartre with their grey shutters and red chimneys and massed pigeons on their roofs.

During one of my visits to Nicole's, I went to Saint-Germain-des-Prés to meet Seppl in her tiny flat, which she has kept since the war years, in Rue du Dragon. She used this pied-à-terre for her occasional trips to Paris from her main residence in Munich, where she and Hubert had settled, when life began to normalise again in Germany, after the war.

I had reunited with Seppl, a few years after my mother's death.

My mother had tried to contact her repeatedly after returning to Europe from New Zealand, only to be confronted every

Portrait of Darius Milhaud by Kortokraks

time with Seppl's steadfast refusal to see or speak with her. When my mother lay dying, in the last days of her life, she kept asking for Seppl. Insistently. There seemed to be something she needed to tell her, unburden herself from, explain... "I want to see Seppl," she would murmur as she emerged briefly out of her dreamy twilight zone. That dark, undefined, inner floating world hovering full with our deepest memories, impressions and sensations spanning all of our existence and reaching back to our origins – the kernel of our being – into which she was sinking with her advancing illness and the heroin she was receiving, during the daily visits from the district nurse to attend to her needs from her increasing incapacitation, wash and tidy her up, and control her pain. "I want to see Seppl," she would say in her soft, weakening voice as she approached death, and "I want to speak to Seppl."

Such is the circuitry of life's experiences and encounters, of the connections and reconnections we stumble upon, that I discovered from an old friend of Kortokraks, who was also Samuel Beckett's German translator, Elmar Tophoven, that he knew Hubert and Seppl all the way back to the early postwar years in Germany. Hubert had died recently, Elmar told me, when I met him and his wife Erika in a villa in Rome's outskirts where they were taking time off. He gave me Seppl's contact details, which I had kept across the years. Watching my mother's desperate deathbed appeals, I decided to use for the first time Elmar's information, to send Seppl the news of my mother's grave illness and her insistent and urgent wish to see her. She only had a few more days to live, I wrote to Seppl.

There was no reply.

It was several years after my mother's death, when I was trying to understand more about her early life, that after some thought, and with some trepidation, I decided to use the

Munich telephone number Elmar had given me.

Seppl answered, and I announced myself in Spanish,

"Soy Miriam, la hija de Käte."

I am Miriam, Käte's daughter.

There was complete silence from the other end of the phone. After the long pause, Seppl exclaimed, her voice quivering with emotion,

"This is astonishing! I was just sitting in my balcony looking at my old photographs of you in La Floresta!"

That was the beginning of our dialogue. She invited me to her home in Munich where I saw her for the first time since our last meeting, when the Spanish Civil War was still raging, and I was a toddler, fifteen months old. In the last photos of Seppl, in the photograph album my mother made of my first years, she is sitting in the sunshine on a deck chair, holding me close to her and pressing her cheek against my little girl cheek,

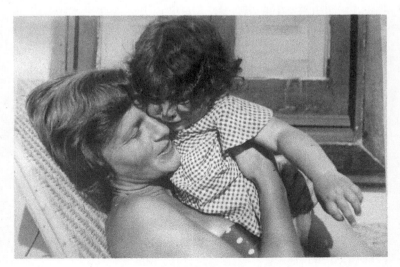

Seppl with Miriam in La Floresta

in the same far corner of the terrace at the entrance of Villa Pepita, where so many photos were taken and I had recently returned to.

At that first meeting in her home in Munich, we spoke at length about her times with my mother in their youth. She told me, too, how she and Hubert had also left Spain and his commitment to the Party and come to France. At the start of the Second World War they had found refuge in a remote area of Haute-Savoie, where Hubert joined the Maquis of the French resistance, and when the war ended they settled in their minimalistic living quarters at the Rue du Dragon, in Paris, down the street from the legendary Le Café de Flore. They became closely involved in the Parisian intellectual scene, which included Somerset Maugham and Gertrude Stein among many others, and Hubert now dedicated himself to his journalism and wrote articles for the new, emerging Germany, with the intention of re-educating the German nation following their recent Nazi past.

Seppl was already in her eighties when we renewed our contact: a slight, warm, hesitant woman masking an underlying strength, her good looks in the photographs still evident.

She had become agitated and her voice tensed when she described their meeting, when Hubert was still alive, with Pavel and Clara Thälmann, at the other renowned Parisian café, La Coupole. The Thälmanns told them that it was my mother who had revealed Hubert's pseudonym in Barcelona.

"She was the only person I had ever confided it to... Disclosing it had placed him in danger of his life!" she had exclaimed nervously.

This was new to me. My mother had rarely mentioned

Seppl and Käte

Hubert, but I had picked up a sense of strong disapproval regarding his mission and work in Spain. And, quite independently, I had received the same response from my father, when I visited him in Mexico.

Seppl and my mother Käte had gone from their soulmate days and shared times together, to finding themselves on opposite sides of a treacherous, menacing divide. The Spanish left had divided into opposing factions: the Thälmanns had taken a stand in the Spanish Civil War on the side of the POUM, the Marxist movement opposed to Stalin's practices. Clara had fought alongside Eric Blair, later to be known as George Orwell, whom she described on one occasion sitting with his gun on a roof close to her barricade and, in her words, "he did not know what was going on and his eyes expressed amazement, he had a terrified look," as he came to realise the deadly split within the Communist Party, in support of which he had come to fight in Spain.

Hubert, on the other hand, was in the Stalinist faction, the PSUC, working at the time in the Catalan government's intelligence department which, in line with Moscow's policies, was denouncing the POUM and the Anarchist organisations as fifth columnists allied to Franco and Hitler.

This was meant to justify the abduction and elimination of its leaders and other prominent members. The head officer in charge of these operations was a Russian known as Aleksander Orlov who, following his infamous purges in Spain in the service of Stalin, defected to the West, when Stalin recalled him to Mosow, fearing that he, in turn, might be next in line in Stalin's purges. Orlov eventually settled in the US and wrote *The Secret History of Stalin's Crimes*, opportunely published in the year of Stalin's death.

My mother, along with so many others, was dismayed at what she was witnessing in what had been, until quite recently, her own Party. The Party she had believed in and thought held so much promise. Now, instead, she passionately disapproved of its activities which included the abduction, interrogation, attempts to extract false confessions, torture, murder and disappearance without trace of people she knew and held in high regard. Those were horrendous times. What for her had started as an idyll in Deià, in the short space of barely two or three years had turned into an unimaginable nightmare. She must have carried this troubling memory with her over the years in her exiled life around the world; it came back to haunt her even in her last hours of life as she lay ill in bed facing her end.

It is a sobering thought to reflect on what is done in the name of an absolute, unbending ideology, in whichever guise – whether political, religious, philosophical, or some other. The total unquestioning commitment, regardless of the human consequences or sacrifice, for what is considered to be the greater good. Along with the power it confers: ideology and power appearing to be two sides of the same coin, one the cerebral counterpart of the other's obsession. And both in direct contradiction and denial of empathy or compassion, those attributes considered the very ultimate in human values.

Seppl spoke to me also of their earlier happier times and of their close friendship, ever since their training days in the children's hospital in Stuttgart, where they first knew each other in their late teens.

"She was *interesting,*" Seppl had remarked about my mother. "She had already experienced much in this world when we met in the *Kinderheim*, and understood more than the rest of us."

She also described with fondness and gratitude how my mother had interrupted her work in New York to return to Barcelona to comfort her and be by her side, on the tragic death of her first husband, Rafael Campalans, after her short marriage.

And I was now visiting Seppl in her Parisian pied-a-terre, from my stopover at Nicole's in Montmartre. Seppl received me in her seventh floor, tiny, one-roomed apartment, with her sofa-bed and books and paintings, and a view over the roofs and chimneys of Paris. It was only a few minutes walk from the Café de Flore: the historical meeting place of Paris's intelligentsia which she and Hubert had frequented during their years here at the end of the war, before returning to Germany and settling into their altogether more opulent and spacious Munich apartment. After our meeting that afternoon, she walked with me to her favourite haunt, Place Furstenberg: a beautiful, classical, leafy square, off a small street behind the Abbey of Saint-Germain-des-Prés, where – she told me in her quiet hesitant voice – she loved to sit and reflect in its peaceful surroundings.

"Would you put some flowers from me on Käte's grave?" she asked when we parted.

Back in London, a low, gloomy sky of heavy rain-bearing clouds is mirrored in the restless river glinting silver as it snakes upriver and round the corner. From my view where I sit, miniature, needle-like boats rowed by teams of tiny men are darting past, followed by their trainers, maybe getting into shape for the annual Oxbridge University Boat Race, and a toy train with an interminable number of carriages is crossing over the railway bridge further upriver.

I am looking at one of my mother's earliest albums. She had not long finished her schooling and was starting to venture out, still in the country of her birth and some years off from her period in England with the Penroses. In this album she has recorded her time in the *Kinderheim* in Stuttgart, dated 1927. A large official photograph shows the hospital: an ivy-covered, three-storey building, with a long, regular row of tall windows stretched across each storey, topped with two more, similar rows protruding through the sloping roof. On the next page there is a group photograph of fifty nurses; I can readily recognise my mother, a tiny figure in the middle of the back row. Seppl begins to appear for the first time in this album, a young slip of a girl with her fine chiselled features and cropped hair, looking relaxed as she sits, in one of the photos, leaning back on top of a fence, outdoors. The photographs in this album are mostly of the children in the hospital; my mother – young and girlish, in her white uniform, her rich dark hair peeping out of her white, nurse's cap – appears totally absorbed and devoted to every single one of her young charges. She fits easily and comfortably into the large sorority of all those young German women embarking into their caring careers on the threshold of their adult life – back in 1927.

She is, here, still on home ground, an integral part of her native surroundings, unaffected as yet by the black storm clouds gathering ominously below the horizon that would soon destroy her future, her happiness and her cherished friendship with Seppl.

Islands' Reflections

We spoke little, often nothing at all – about what was going on and determining our lives – my mother and I. Her focus, all of her time and attention, were fully taken up in juggling our survival and meeting our essential needs with her long hours of work and everything else our continually changing circumstances demanded of her.

Our exchanges would switch from closely engaged and communicative to increasingly absent and disconnected. In France, after we left La Floresta when Franco's armies were closing in, she drew on all her energy and resources to keep us alive and avoid capture when the next more global and cataclysmal war erupted. After she had managed to extricate us from occupied France, under its collaborating Vichy regime, she took on day and night jobs to keep a roof over our heads, and for my education, in Mexico. And a few years later, by then in New Zealand, she set about once again readjusting to another entirely different way of life, with new work, friends and commitments. We never recovered our time together, mother and daughter, in La Floresta. Instead, we faced a difficult world the best we could, each largely to herself, and she taught me self-reliance and self-sufficiency from an early age.

The Cycladic island of Serifos, in the Aegean Sea
I have returned to this island where the sun and sea clear my thoughts and empty the clutter of undigested impressions we are bombarded with from so many sources, whether from the

exterior world or from our own, often overloaded and under-charged, internal one.

There are many sites on the island where I find peace and inspiration, close to the raw elements. A favourite is Agios Sostis, along the southeast coast, not far from the Chora. A rocky strip of land with a small white church in the middle sep-arates two bays off a single sweep of beach. When the wind blows from the north, the sea is rough and choppy in the more exposed open bay, in stark contrast to the other, deeper cove, where it stretches blue and satin smooth. Four ancient tamarisk trees throw their refreshing shade at this end of the beach, from where I like to swim across the transparently clear, unruf-fled water to the steps that lead up to the church on the other side of the cove. Here, I scramble on the rocks in my bare feet, climbing up and down and in and out amongst the huge boul-ders, to finally emerge into the wild spraying and frothing of the thundering waves crashing against the cliff face below me, on the headland's furthest point.

Today I went swimming with my friend Panos from Athens, who also has a summer house here, close to mine, at the top of the Chora. The strong, northern winds have calmed down, so we chose a beach in the north coast. We drove across the middle of the island, climbing to the highest point of the road and coming down steeply on the other side, through some hairpin curves, past the village of Panagia with its tiny ancient Byzantine church, a few fig trees laden with fruit by the side of the road further on, the large imposing white monastery inhab-ited by a single remaining monk along with his rafter of white turkeys, to finally wind our way down a jerky dirt road, past the ruins of a deserted old settlement from another age near the top, and a few newer, holiday residences lower down, till we reached the sea.

Here, in Platis Gialos, there is a small white church on raised ground, a simple taverna that serves its own homegrown produce on its terrace overlooking the sea, and three small coves. As we face the shore with its crystalline waters, the one on the left is long, open and shallow with a few fishermen's huts and boats at the far end. A rocky promontory that juts out into the sea separates it from the middle one, which is small and intimate and shaded by an ancient, spreading tamarisk tree. The third, to our right, is reached after a short walk along a scrubby goat track. This is where we head. As we reach the end of the track where it turns into a steep descent, we pause for a moment to look down at the pristine empty beach covered in white pebbles and dry seaweed, with the crystal clear turquoise sea blending into blue as it stretches out of the bay. No one else in view. And no trees – the only shade being provided by some overhanging rocks on the far side of the beach which, to keep us cool, we shall follow as the sun moves with the hours.

We leave our bags with our clothes, books, sun lotion and towels in the shade under the rocks and run into the water. It is cool and fresh, sparkling and limpid, on this windless day. Panos has a shortish dip and then scrambles out again for a wander along the higher ground behind the beach to forage through the arid vegetation and stony terrain with its rich and colourful mineral specimens, occasionally also coming across unexpected artefacts that have lain disregarded and undetected from the island's past cultures and inhabitants down the ages. I, instead, continue to swim out, stroke after cool easy stroke, looking into the transparent water as it plunges beneath me, at first into the light sandy seabed alternating with darker irregular patches of seaweed and sea life while, further out, as the seafloor continues to fall away, into a deep blue void. Between my strokes, arcing forward and sweeping back against the water, I am taking in the view all around me as I leave behind the bay's rocky enclosure and the diminishing white beach beyond the watery blue expanse that now separates us. I slice through the water and feel it rippling against my body all about me. Out here – at this moment in time – the sea, the sky and I are one.

The Frisian island of Helgoland, in the North Sea

My mother was starting out in life, fresh out of school, back in the mid-1920s. She spent time and found work in Berlin, and would holiday on the island of Helgoland, off the northern coast of Germany. Days of swimming, fresh air, gymnastics, flirting and fun with like-minded friends.

Helgoland and Serifos, in their altogether different seas and times, share much in common. Both islands are separated from their countries' mainland by a similar stretch of sometimes turbulent waters.

They both present a rugged, untamed landscape that awakens a close connection with nature and the raw elements, and both have drawn and inspired people seeking freedom from social constraints and conventions, and a respite from urban life. An emerging naturism, healthy body culture and sexual and gender freedoms were voguish trends in avant-garde circles of early twentieth-century Germany. Helgoland, with its beautiful wild beaches and surroundings, became a natural haunt for them – much as one finds in Serifos today. And, like

Käte on her way to Helgoland in heavy seas

Mallorca's Deià, Helgoland has attracted writers, poets, composers and painters. Film makers too have used its striking

rocky landscape to stage the backdrop for their films, dating back to some of the earliest classic German cinema, such as *Nosferatu*, in which Alexander Granach played a leading part – and would play a leading role also in my mother's life – and *The Holy Mountain*, with Leni Riefenstahl, before Hitler discovered her – the tall cliffs and wild sea enhancing the exalted dramatic effects.

The photos in my mother's album dedicated to Helgoland show seascapes under moody skies with churning foaming tides crashing against rocks and a stony shore. Low houses with angular roofs line the town's straight cobbled streets. My mother is with a group of friends doing the then fashionable German gymnastics on the beach. In one photograph she stands daringly and triumphantly at the top of a human tower. In others, a male dancer poses in loose clothing, barefoot, in an expressionist stance, or is trying on a girl's dress. Two slim young female friends are silhouetted naked, twisting their fingers into whimsical positions against a moonlit sea, while over the page local old women, in their head scarves and ankle-length skirts and aprons, sit in doorways with their knitting on their laps. A sharp, black and white photograph shows the small distant figures of bathers spread across a swelling surfing sea, swathed in froth.

The young Käte, in her late teens here, appears to be launching into this free, liberal lifestyle, breaking away from the conventional background in which she had been brought up by her conservative parents, in their assimilated German Jewish household, and their circle of friends, in the industrial town of Chemnitz. She was growing into a modern, emancipated young woman of the age.

Gymnasts in the moonlight in Helgoland

She had finished school and not yet started her nurse training in Stuttgart, when she decided to sample life in Berlin where she could test her emerging independence. She stayed at her aunt Martha's, a rather squat and stern older sister of her mother Clara, who lived in a flat in a street off the Kurfüstendamm with her son and his young bride, Friedel. My mother and Friedel became close friends and confidantes. She started working with children, her interest and passion, at the progressive educational centre, Pestalozzi Fröbel Haus, while she savoured the bohemian ambience of the great city. Her brother Fritz, my uncle, once told me that she would have liked to go to university, but as much as her father doted on his beloved youngest daughter Käte, he would not entertain the idea: higher education was for men, women were prepared for the chores of a household and marriage.

When, some two years later, she completed her paediatric nurse training at the *Kinderheim* in Stuttgart, she returned to

Berlin where she worked privately with eminent specialists and in children's clinics, and plunged back into the sophisticated intellectual and artistic life of the city – a world buzzing with its new forms of Bauhaus architecture, expressionist art, cinema, dance and theatre, Brecht and Weill, of mordant burlesque cabaret that mixed sharp political satire with bold and explicit sensuality and sexuality. The new talkies were becoming popular and she had a deep admiration for the actor Elisabeth Bergner, whose elegantly nuanced roles – ranging from tender and fragile to femme fatale, from an imperial queen to androgynous – she idolised, Seppl told me during our conversations when we met again after my mother's death. Maybe it was Bergner's assertive expression of the freedom of her gender, her strength and independence, along with a certain intimate sweetness and vulnerability, that appealed to the young Käte.

As the twenties advanced, she also became inevitably drawn and actively involved in the mounting political unrest and sharp divisions that were spreading across the German Weimar Republic of the interwar years, and were now threatening the famed metropolis. Here, preceding her time in Spain, the broad spectrum of left wing ideologies, from socialists, democrats, liberal and social democrats, through to the various dissenting variants of communism, were in constant and often violent conflict with each other, with the Stalinists jostling for leading position through their abstruse strategies and physical elimination of their opponents. Though this was becoming common practice across the board, and hit close to home with the assassination of my grandfather's cousin, Hugo Haase – who had led the more conciliatory, pacific branch of the social democrats – as he stood on the front steps of the *Reichstag* in Berlin. At the other end of the spectrum, the National Socialist German Workers' Party was ruled by a bunch of fanatic thugs, headed by a fierce, at that stage often ridiculed, humourless character with a trim moustache, a shrill grating voice, and as yet little power, though spreading growing fear and terror in the streets, and gathering an increasing momentum of followers.

In the midst of all this, the young blossoming Käte was also having various amorous adventures. Many young men were falling in love with her and she received several proposals of marriage, to which she would reply, "But I can't cook!"

The Galician actor, Alexander Granach, who was with the *Deutsches Theater* in Berlin at the time, appears to have been captivated by her. In a passionate love scene he was playing in the theatre, she would hear him from her seat in the front row whisper her name under his breath on the stage while he was embracing his paramour in the play. She was some fourteen years younger than him, and seems not to have fully matched his feelings at the time, but their deep friendship and affection for each other grew with time and survived their divergent paths and commitments, as they continued to exchange letters and news when the forthcoming wars and circumstances allowed.

I remember mail arriving for my mother from Alexander when we had settled in Mexico and he, in turn, had emigrated to the United States, after an intervening period in the Soviet Union where he narrowly escaped the Gulag. He was, by then, following his acting career in New York and Hollywood, and appeared in films such as Ernst Lubitsch's *Ninotchka*, Fritz

Lang's *Hangmen also Die!* and *For Whom the Bell Tolls* after Hemingway's novel, until his premature death, which I remember threw my mother into profound grieving.

She left behind some of his letters, in which he always addressed her fondly, *Meine geliebte Katinka*, and responded to the difficulties in her life – which she must have confided in her correspondence with him – trying to uplift her spirits with wise counsel and tenderness. But these were sporadic communications from distant countries that ended abruptly when he died from complications following emergency surgery.

For all of my mother's admirers and lovers, she appears never to have had a fulfilling relationship or a lasting love. Or someone to share her dispersed life and homes.

What *is* home? A geographical site, the place of your birth where you grew up surrounded by family and friends, as familiar and as much a part of you as the palm of your hand. Or is it a state of mind?

Maybe it is made up of all our memories, added to the customs and culture we have grown up with and which have become ingrained in us, along with the language and a way of thinking, all of which becomes in-built and mixed and modified with the further experience of new worlds – culminating in a portable, integrated home. One we carry with us everywhere we go.

After a lifetime of rootless and homeless wandering, I feel at home on the island of Serifos. A place where I can be myself, after years of alteration and adaptation from one culture, language and people, to another. After years also of studies and work and application – all of which has been enriching, if sometimes arduous and difficult. Here, now, in Serifos, I can spend lazy days reading, writing, swimming and going for walks.

I also take pleasure in the company of neighbours and new friends I have made on the island.

My nearest neighbours are Josette and Frangiscus. Their white cubic house is a few steps down the path on the other side of the ancient gate into the Kastro. It faces East, from where the fierce Meltemi winds blow, with an extensive view over the Aegean. We often sit in the small, sheltered courtyard at the back of their house, sipping iced ouzo and picking at the island's olives and Josette's hors d'oeuvres, facing the sheer rockface that drops from the summit, and the white stone steps to their dovecote built into the rock. As the evening advances, we continue our pre-dinner conversation to the light of a flickering candle, until it is time to leave this pleasant corner in their patio and move inside to continue our talk over Josette's gourmet Parisian cuisine: likely to include fish that Frangiscus fetched, by foot, from the port, when the fishermen came in with their catch, as the sun was rising.

Josette comes from a deeply conservative Parisian household and, like my mother, broke away from their traditional values. She went on to take an active part in the *événements*, of the 1960s and 70s, with Cohn-Bendit and his group. As we sit and chat, I observe she has retained the good looks of her youth, in the photograph displayed on the antique cabinet in their living room: her raven black hair now a snowy white mass swept into a large knot on the back of her head, its whiteness accentuating her dark, fiery eyes.

Frangiscus is retired from his work as the Greek correspondent of the BBC World Service in London, and later in Paris, where he met Josette. He is the son of an aristocratic family descended from the Crusaders who settled in Naxos, his native island. Although his family still own the great medieval castle overlooking the main town and port in Naxos, Frangiscus became devoted since his early youth to socialism; he stood against Fascism during the Second World War and fought in the Greek Civil War that followed.

Josette's and Frangiscus's stories, diverse as they are from each other and from mine, also share much common ground with mine. Their backgrounds abound with echoes of my own. Frangiscus's role and commitment in the Greek Civil War seemed to parallel my mother's experience in Spain, though from there on they diverged. My mother and her circle became disillusioned with the ideology they had once embraced, while Josette and Frangiscus's loyalty has continued up till today.

Our evening meal winds down to the sounds of rare gems from Frangiscus's collection of old-time music in the bars and brothels in Turkey. The poignant singing and deeply stirring renditions, sound to me like the Judeo-Greco-Turkish equivalent of a Billy Holiday.

Josette and Frangiscus form part of a strong French presence on Serifos. I enjoy also the company of Marc and Sylvie Sator, who come from Paris every summer to stay in a small hotel in the headland of the port. I have shared evenings of lively talk over a Greek meal with them, listening to their stories of their great collection of André Breton's estate, which they manage and curate in Paris.

This takes me back to Mexico, where I remember my

mother's work, soon after we arrived, with the Austrian artist Wolfgang Paalen, to whose great, Coyoacan home and garden, full of tropical plants and pre-Columbian artefacts, I sometimes accompanied her. Before his exile to Mexico, Paalen had lived in Paris and been closely involved with Breton and the surrealist movement. And now, on Serifos, I was reconnecting with that early part of my life through the Sators. Home, then, is also the meeting point of all that relates with one's self.

Both the landscape and seascape, the sights and sounds, and the people on this island make me feel grounded, at home.

From the top of a mountain ridge, I look back at the collection of white cubes that make up the Chora cluttered on the hillside against the lapis lazuli sea, with the clear outline of the neighbouring island of Sifnos rising out of the water. Further out, the more distant, fuzzy form of Milos – once home to the marble effigy of Venus – stretches out into a long, low-lying, mantle over the sea. On a clear day I can make out the whole ring of outlying islands across the Aegean: Syros, Tinos, Mykonos, Paros, Naxos, Folegandros, and sometimes even more, as faint, distant, discrete forms floating above the horizon.

With new friends on the island, or old ones that are on a visit, we dine at Maria's sitting under the cicada laden tamarisk trees, lined along the seafront of the old mining town of Megalivadi, in the west of the island, or at Margarita's at the far end of the long beach in the main port. Both women serve their own, freshly picked produce cooked into the local dishes. One night, sitting at a table in Margarita's large homely kitchen, we were treated to a spontaneous outburst of Balkan music from a group sitting at the next table, transporting us to another land and age with their nostalgic, ancient traditional songs...

Here, on this island in the Mediterranean, I have an atavistic sense of our ancient history and peoples and civilisation. A sense of continuity across the ages, right down to me now.

Home is where I am comfortable and feel at one with my surroundings.

Or with someone who feels close.

When I first met Kortokraks, we felt a deep rapport, a mutual understanding and shared experiences and views of the world. I found him inspirational, and he could be gentle, warm and empathic. He immediately set to draw me and paint me, while I was learning, through him, more about myself and my own past.

We formed a strong, instinctive bond, felt most deeply during our tender moments, when he held me close, in the dead of night, free from daily thoughts and anxieties. When we felt as one.

Yet, back in the daylight and the practicalities of everyday life, misapprehensions and conflicts, the push and pull of overwhelming demands that defied any logic, and so much more that has been handed down from painful experiences and traumas in the past, would start to get in the way. And arguments would spark, understanding and dialogue vanish, and smarting and hurting replace caring and empathy.

The nature of love in its myriad guises is a never-ending mystery. How much of it is illusionary, how much is it a mirror of our yearning imagination, how much based on our concep-

tion or misconception of reality, based on our particular circumstances and needs, at that moment in our lives, for idolatry,
or simply a companion? It may take hold as a jealous desire to
possess exclusively, along with its ensuing destructive trail, or
conversely as the unconditional striving for the other's happiness and wellbeing, regardless of the cost to oneself. And all
the phases in between. And then, with it or beyond it, there is
friendship, devotion and loyalty, spanning across every kind of
appreciation, support and sharing, through to disillusion,
deception and treachery... I remember D H Lawrence talking
through Gudrun and Ursula in his *Women in Love*, which would
have been written around the years of my mother's vacations
in Helgoland, exploring love in its various forms and finally
finding it in the sharing together, with passion, yet without for-
feiting each other's separateness.

I recall the occasional comments I would hear from my
mother, not addressed especially to me but more as though
expressing her thoughts out loud, which I as a child would take
in and think about and tuck away as part of my armamentari-
um for life. Although in principle she seemed to believe in and
was comfortable with a free, non-possessive love, when it came
to its motherly version, or to me, it seemed more difficult to
put it into practice, to let go and watch me grow independent
from her: she would misinterpret diminished need as diminished love. When it came to my father's love affairs, aside from
the painful deception by one or two of her close female
friends, she did not reproach his lovers – some of whose
adoring letters she had come across – but felt rather a kind of
sisterly sympathy for their predicament, and pity for their rosy,
idealised view of him. Which I expect she must have also

entertained once, before her longer association and disillusion.

I remember her commenting on the wording of a popular Mexican song, the kind the Mariachis accompanied, suggesting one should rely more on myth and imagination and less on a rigid naked truth, if one is to retain one's love and prevent it from fading, and she – with her Prussian Jewish upbringing of which something had remained with her – remarked on the native insight and wisdom to be found in these songs, which might appear deceptively simple and lowbrow, but were full of a raw basic understanding of love, life and death, joy, grief and treachery in all their shades and variations.

I am writing here about my mother, and yet my image of her is inevitably distorted by my view and feelings about her. I see her through my own coloured spectacles, or rather the lenses inbuilt into my eyes, an indivisible part of me. I may manage to capture something of her past life and experiences, of her ethos and mood, as surely as I was born from her and our identities once merged – yet I am also aware of much about her I cannot grasp or comprehend, just as she could not penetrate a significant part of my own make-up.

As stoical and independent a figure as she cut, and as forward looking and acting as she was prone to be, she must have carried some wounds and hurt deep inside her which, however well hidden, I suspect never healed.

Even so, her multiple uprooting and sense of dislocation did not hold her back. In every new place, she met and threw herself into the challenges of adapting and making a new life and forming new connections. Her home was where she found herself; she created her own congenial and familiar ambience in every new country, with her books and photographs, art works and music, cherished objects from her past worlds and life, and new lasting friendships. Home is where you make it and recreate it.

In my house in Serifos, I have books on the history of Byzantium, Italy, and Europe, on Greek legends and art, and of Sappho's poetry. And Isaac Bashevis Singer's stories, in which his two contrasting worlds – life in an Eastern European shtetl and in the glass and concrete jungle of Manhattan – bring me closer to my father as I try to understand his early life in a rural, farming, Orthodox Jewish community in the outskirts of a village in Lithuania, abruptly switched with that of an immigrant child growing into adulthood in a crowded tenement building on the Lower East side of New York and on Manhattan's West Side.

Hand-painted and fired bowls and plates from Tunisia and Morocco, and hand-woven Indian throws and bedspreads, also adorn my Greek island house. Here East and West overlap and merge, just as I too come from and share both sides of that divide.

The land becomes greener and more fertile in the valley that runs into the port. Bright cherry red and magenta bougainvillea against white walls and a deep blue sky, a plethora of prickly pear and other cacti, tall bamboos and the occasional donkey bring Mexico, and my childhood, back to me.

In the spring, the countryside comes alive everywhere with wild flowers, red and yellow poppies, white Queen Anne's lace, chamomile daisies with their rich orange centres, a ground-spread of deep blue bugloss, tall thistles with their bulging bulbous purple buds. Bordering paths and through cracks between the rocks, blue-green caper plants drape their dense round foliage, lifting their delicate white flowers with their violet tipped filaments bunched and splayed in their centre.

All this is home to me – close to nature, free from man's national, factional, and other controversial and contested boundaries. Out of reach from deceit and deception, false judgement or prejudice.

Islands are finite places that give a sense of containment within. They also serve as areas of refuge from the larger land mass, with its jumble of human complexities and contradictions. Their geographic isolation and watery encirclement encourage a sense of tranquillity and communion with nature.

My mother appears to have found this in Deià. Along with love, beauty, inspiration, comradeship and happiness. She had left and lost forever her native home, her family and friends, her basic roots and familiar milieu, and readjusted to her new life in Barcelona and Deià.

My mother's memories of Mallorca, in her life of exile across oceans and continents, evoked a magic world in my imagination, which drew me to visit the island soon after I returned to Europe from New Zealand. My own impressions of Deià fitted her nostalgic recollections, and I returned with Kortokraks and my first-born, Rebekah, and again during my pregnancy with my second child, Anna – just as my mother had also been there with me inside her.

More recently I revisited Mallorca in my attempts to retrace her steps. I took her albums with Deià's photographs, hoping to find someone who may still remember her and Seppl, but the one or two people from that time who are still there, were too advanced in age to recognise them.

The village's irrepressible beauty never ceases to stir and inspire me, yet the great increase in tourism has inescapably altered the equilibrium of earlier years between humankind and nature. Robert Graves made his home, wrote his poetry and literary works, and lived out his life here; he is buried in the churchyard at the summit of the village, and his house has been turned into a museum. In the main street, a large choice of cafés and restaurants have sprung up and added international cuisine to their menus, and boutiques sell from Mallorcan to Parisian, Peruvian, Indian and Malaysian articles and clothing. People arrive to attend workshops on art and creative writing, and for healthy living and detoxifying courses. Richard Branson had four great residences turned into a sumptuous hotel, La Residencia, now owned by the Orient-Express and frequented by Hollywood and British celebrities, and Andrew Lloyd Webber has bought the side of a mountain on which he has built his retreat.

Even so, though Deià has moved forward, I still found a direct link with my mother's life when I visited and was invited to stay with the present owners of Villa Pepita, at their home in Palma, Mallorca. Dino Ibanez and his wife Dolors Juncosa knew the previous proprietors of Villa Pepita and spoke to me of the history of the house, touching close to the time when my mother and I lived there. They welcomed and treated me like a member of the family, and our amazing link through Villa Pepita added a strong emotional undertone to our meeting, which made me too feel as though I had discovered some long lost distant relatives. I felt at home with Dino and Dolors.

Stewart Island, in the Antipodes

On the other side of the world, wedged between the Tasman and South Pacific Seas, is New Zealand's third and southern-most island, Stewart Island. It is known also by its earlier name of *Rakiura*, Maori for The Land of the Glowing Skies.

New Zealand is where we arrived after sailing across two oceans, within my first twelve years of life: the Atlantic, from Marseilles to Veracruz, when I was a young child, and the Pacific, from San Francisco to Auckland, when I was entering puberty.

It was a long way from my mother's Mallorca and Helgoland days, and from those islands' pre-war, libertarian and permissive ambience. The New Zealand my mother found in the middle of the twentieth century was genteel and conservative in its traditions, left over from the British pioneers who had not so long before peopled these islands from Victorian England. There were no free expressions of sensuality, or nude dancing scenes on the beach: here women wore pastel shaded twin sets and calf length skirts, and nobody ever, but ever, touched in public. There was definitely no kissing or hugging; people didn't even ever shake hands. But neither had New Zealand gone through the political upheaval, decimation and carnage that had recently convulsed Europe, and everyone we came across was the personification of kindness, generosity and hospitality, in contrast to the injustice and stark cruelty we had left behind.

After an initial difficult period – a mix of great excitement and joy at her reunion with her sister and family, along with renewed hardships as she started rebuilding her life in this new country, followed by a spell of acute depression – my mother settled into her new life. She soon made friendships with members of the Christchurch intelligentsia, which formed part of her sister Lotte's circle.

Lotte's migration to New Zealand, when the Second World War broke out in Europe, was facilitated by a German couple, Paul and Ottilie Binswanger, whom she knew from her years in Florence, and who arrived shortly before her. Lotte settled into her new home, round the corner from the Binswangers, in Christchurch. Paul was a scholar of literature who was being watched by New Zealand's secret intelligence when it was discovered that he wrote letters, with carbon copies, in a foreign language, and that he consorted with Pacifists, while Otti took certain sections of Christchurch by storm with her rhythmic gymnastics, which she brought over from her Berlin-in-the-Twenties days, and she was convinced was the right antidote to the local population's repressed Victorian character.

Friends in this lively group included Margaret Birkinshaw with her two daughters, one of whom would emerge years later as the author Fay Weldon, as well as the local artists, poets, writers and intellectuals who sought the controversial and non-conformist in this generally placid and conforming society. These members of the cultural scene in Christchurch, befriended by Lotte and the Binswangers, and whom my mother encountered on her arrival to New Zealand, were part of a group that was acutely conscious of the isolation of their country, both geographically and culturally, while at the same time was establishing its own character and particularity with its evolving art and literature. These writers and artists were naturally attracted by the worldly outlook and culture these refugees brought with them from old Europe. Some formed part of the university's English Department, and my mother forged strong friendships with several of its staff. Professor Winston Rhodes was a convinced communist – a courageous stance, here in this faraway, conservative corner of the world, though one my mother had discarded following her own, first-hand experiences in Spain. Other individual members in the department who formed close ties with my mother were part of the gay literary circle in Christchurch, who in the climate of those times could not come out. They must have found her like a breath of fresh air bearing the scent and seeds from an era and world known to them mostly through the literature and poetry they knew and loved from the books they studied.

Her life soon found and settled into its new rhythm, and her friendships here too – as in all the other countries she had lived and loved in – became close and enduring.

Ironically, the only cog that would not fit into this new system was also her strongest connection to that earlier part of her life that represented the turning point from a happy care-free period to a painful and difficult struggle for survival: me. She couldn't find a way to include me in her new life in New Zealand where, in my emerging adolescence, I had become a stranger to her. Or so she imagined and resented and raged against.

Meantime, I was going through high school, trying to fit in and adapt to a new language, unfamiliar customs and different outlooks from my friendly but remote peers. I enjoyed their company and sharing our school activities with them, but – deep down inside me – some connection was missing and I felt very alone in their midst.

When I go to New Zealand today, I get a warm welcome from my old high school classmates, whom I recently met again after a lifetime of divergent experiences. I came across Sally in London, whom I remembered as always gentle and patient with me in my foreign ways, when we went through high school together, including her time as head prefect, when she would have had reason to admonish my problem with adhering to the traditionally British school rules. Through Sally, I reconnected with other classmates. Of these, Jill – a lively and bubbly teenager when we last met – invited me to stay at her home, when I was recently back in New Zealand to take part in the Christchurch Writers Festival. And in the way life has of springing surprises and coincidences, tying loose ends together in the most unexpected ways, I found myself staring through the window in the lovely cosy room Jill had prepared for me, at Lotte's house across the road, our first home when we arrived in New Zealand from Mexico all those years ago. Many of the houses and gardens and fences in Rugby Street had changed, but Lotte's was still the same, though now painted a dark, murky shade of mustard, which somehow fitted my conflicting and not very happy memories of my arrival and first months in that house. My room at Jill's now, and our room at Lotte's then, were not only a lifetime apart, but also a world apart in form of welcome.

Jill organised a moving reunion with our old classmates, Leona, with whom I had been having a moving correspondence from London, Judith and Pam. We caught up with one another over lunch – their voices, mannerisms and characters tugging at and unplugging my memories of them when we were in our early teens and just starting off in life, while our connection and exchanges now reflected the growing insights that our lives have taught us. I now get an affectionate hug from them when we meet again. With the passage of years, facilitated travel, and the digital communication explosion, the restraint and reserve of those times is as much in their past as in mine. They tell me they remember me as a bright, lively and happy young girl. And I was indeed full of fun; I was sporty, studious, playful, and high-spirited.

And yet, had anyone scratched a little deeper they would have found an insecure, confused, adolescent girl who felt very much alone in a new country, struggling to find something in common with her peers. My mother seemed caught up with her own problems following this latest move, and had grown increasingly distant from me. Her previous caring and consideration had been replaced with cold disapproval, and our communication reduced to scolding and criticising. I had lost her loving support during our previous uprootings, as well as everything else that I had grown familiar and close to. My language too, that in which I used to express myself, in which I thought and felt and communicated, I had had to sever from my neural networks in my brain and replace with a whole new system in my thinking and formulation.

For one who has had to hold at bay so many difficulties and concerns, at what seemed a safe distance from where they wouldn't graze or touch or burn or hurt too much, held too from where those feelings might be prevented from getting out of control, for one who has managed to keep a semblance of

wellness and brightness over inner layers of struggles and disconnection, now - after the greater part of a lifetime felt and
handled, however tenuously at times, with what strength and
determination can be rallied - this demonstration of a deep
affection, interest and caring, from a group of girls once seem-
ingly at root so alien, is very comforting and heartening.

Now, in my renewed friendship with my classmates from
Christchurch Girls High School, I find their sense of loyalty
and solidarity, in a group of girls who once seemed so unlike
me, and I to them, very precious. An affirmation of a deep-
seated commonality that joins people of every background and
station in life. Given a chance.

While still a schoolgirl in Christchurch, I used to go out
walking at the weekends with another girl my age, whom I met
at a "church social" – the only other gathering of young
people, besides my school, where I could mix and make new
friends at the time. She enjoyed hiking in the Port Hills that rise
where the flat sweep of land on which Christchurch was built
ends, to descend on the other side into Lyttelton Harbour. I no
longer recall her name but I can see in remarkable detail her
disarmingly frank smile, as we climbed over the rough and
rocky terrain, all the while exchanging our thoughts and ideas
in the immediacy of the moment and our surroundings – just
the two of us under the sky, clouds and sun in that rugged hilly
landscape of tussock and native vegetation.

Despite our radically different backgrounds and experiences – she had grown up naturally, healthily and unhampered
by conflict or adversity in New Zealand and knew nothing
outside it, while I all the contrary – out here we connected fully

and easily, without obstacles or complications. Our hikes were the high point of my week. They ended when I left Christchurch for Dunedin to attend the only medical school in New Zealand at the time.

The study of medicine, the learning of what up till then was known on how the body and mind work, and of how to assist healing and bring relief in the face of illness and injury, seemed to answer my attempts at understanding my own inner turmoil, along with my desire to prevent and relieve suffering in others.

When I started university in Dunedin, I joined the Varsity Tramping Club. Hiking out in the wild and beautiful native bush, I became whole and happy here again. I felt thoroughly at peace and at home with my surroundings in this lush Antipodean nature.

In my first year, a group of us went on a four day Easter tramping trip to Stewart Island: a thickly forested, sparsely populated island with a rich native vegetation and bird life, on the furthest point of the Antipodes. A stark contrast with the Mediterranean islands, with their terraced olive groves, a turquoise sea, and a hot sun. Or from Helgoland in the North Sea.

We set off from Half Moon Bay, with its scattering of wooden lodges; the whole group had slept in one of these the night before, in a shared room, in our sleeping bags. We started hiking in the early morning along the coastline. Our heavy packs on our backs – carrying our sleeping bags and cover, a parka, change of clothes and boots, plate and mug, soap and toothbrush – we marched single file through the thick vegetation of native trees, ferns, climbers and mosses, which crowded the moist fertile ground and created a magical roofed-in world of greens. We climbed up and down the steep undulating terrain, fording the small clear streams of pure, icy, spring water, which quenched our thirst at the bottom of each descent. We heard the flutelike, ping-pong call of the bellbird and the rare trill of the tui, with the occasional fleeting glimpse, through the thick foliage, of its glossy blue-green feathers. At the end of the long day's trek across twenty miles, we put up tents, made a wood fire, and sat around it, chatting and relaxed, eating our meal of sausages and tinned peas before retiring to a deep, sound sleep inside our warm sleeping bags, our backs relieved from our packs' heavy weight.

The following morning we dived from the rocks and swam in the sea's transparent icy water above clustered colonies of colourful iridescent pauas, which provided a delicious breakfast of abalone shellfish. As we trudged back again steadily and rhythmically up the coast through the native bush, we were surrounded by a profusion of ferns in every shape and form: from dainty uncurling fresh green shoots at the base of trees and bushes, to bunching sprays of graceful arching fronds, on to tall tree-ferns, their giant radial fronds spread out widely, umbrella-like, from the top of their thick, stepped trunks, into a luxuriant canopy of green feathery lace. Long strings of silvery green, old man's beard hung from native trees everywhere before us, and the song or call from a native bird would break out above the quiet, monotonous crunching of our boots on the stony track. And here again: I felt comfortable, in my element, at home, losing myself and blending into my surroundings with a deep sense of harmony.

In contrast, back at my mother's home in Christchurch

during the university term break, the bitter hostility and clashes that had risen and grown between us here in New Zealand, went on. The fragmentary rapport with my peers, from our divergent backgrounds, was trivial compared with my confusion and disorientation at the relentless censure from a mother who had once been so close and supportive.

This was no ordinary strife between mother and adolescent daughter. Others remarked on it. One mild-mannered, elderly, academic refugee broke off in the middle of his friendly conversation with my mother over what had been, up till then, a pleasant and peaceful afternoon tea in his charming garden, at his home in the foothills of Christchurch, and in a sudden and uncharacteristic fit of fury sharply reprehended her for the way she was reprimanding me over some simple comment I had made while we were having tea. It made a huge impression on me. I had become accustomed to her attacks as a matter of course and it never occurred to me that anyone might object to them on my behalf. Helmut, moreover, was my mother and my aunt Lotte's friend; to me, he seemed a genteel, always courteous, and rather remote figure who discussed philosophical questions with the adults. My mother was completely taken aback by his furious defence of me; she responded meekly and falteringly, attempting to justify herself, but she soon regained her composure and put it behind her.

More recently, the daughter of a local family we lodged with, after our initial time at my aunt Lotte's, and with whom we were in close everyday contact during my high school years, told me when we met on one of my visits to New Zealand:

"It used to upset me to see how Käte treated you. My parents tried to reason with her, but it didn't help."

All of which made me think.

Maybe, I wondered, the extreme uncertainties we had lived through when we faced life-threatening dangers in warring Europe, and we only had each other, had intensified our closeness and tightened our bond. Now, as she watched me grow into a separate person, reaching out into new spheres of my own, beyond her reach and milieu, she may have been feeling profoundly let down. Perhaps abandoned? Betrayed, even. Maybe she was afraid of losing me – her little girl – and all we had meant to each other in those difficult times.

Only now is it beginning to dawn on me that during our moves from one place to another, within countries and across continents, evading capture and seeking safety, she would have needed me as much as I depended on her. She described on several occasions her terrifying ordeal when she was caught by the German military police on her way to collect me from my father's quarters in the occupied zone: one couldn't help but be impressed by the cool, level-headed courage that helped her extricate herself from her captors and interrogators. More than I being saved by her, maybe my presence and love and need of her was saving her, giving her the strength, motivation and unswerving perseverance she needed to save us both. She had been the centre of my universe; up till now I hadn't recognised the importance of my being the centre of hers too.

And now I was changing, I was no longer her fiercely close and dependent little girl that she had come to rely on. She failed to recognise that my love and constancy were as strong as ever, but changing along with my own changing self from child to adult and all the altering perspectives that entails.

And I, in turn, felt let down by her, disturbed and bewildered by her anger. It would break me up into a thousand disparate pieces that would grate and chafe and lacerate me inside and make me lose sight of myself, much more than the sum of all our losses and our many different homes. My mother was my home: she had been the one constant presence in a forever changing world. Our unshakable closeness had given me the assurance and confidence that one would otherwise acquire from one's roots and nation. And now, the same person whose love and approval had been so affirming when I was a small growing child, was pronouncing quite the reverse. That, more than all else, was at the root of my sense of dispossession.

But it also turned into one more challenge for me to overcome and emerge from with renewed strength.

And, above all else, it was in my moments of communion with nature that I recovered my whole, serene self again. To become immersed in the lush native bush; rugged rocks against turquoise sea and blue sky; the intense illumination of the moon; the monotonous swelling, retreating and crashing of the waves against the seashore...

And sometimes, being held close and fast, wordlessly, sinking deeply into our primal state, with a full sense of mutual trust and acceptance.

The Sun and the Moon and this Earth

At my London city apartment, the changing skies and astonishing sunsets – wondrous displays that touch us all – make me feel at home here too.

My home is where I find inner peace. Where I can take off my shoes that stepped on the more uncertain and precarious world outside, and slip into my comfortable slippers in surroundings I have made my own, with the things I love and of my choosing. A niche where I can drop all masks and be my own, unapologetic, natural self. My own personal island, to which I can retreat from the bigger, more complicated and challenging world out there, in all its intriguing variations and configurations.

I am leaning against the glass railing on my terrace, the Thames shimmering below me, today's bright summer sunlight bouncing off its flickering surface flashing quicksilver from every ruffle. The sun bears down on the terrace deck enveloping me in its warmth and making me feel at one with the world. The same sun that gladdens and heartens me also on a beach in Serifos. Though surrounded by rocks, cacti and white cubic houses in one, and steel-and-glass constructions next to Victorian bricks-and-mortar in the other – the sky and the sun and the suffusion of light and warmth they invoke, create one and the same sensation and state of being.

It is the sun and the moon and this earth that instil a sense of fit and harmony and make us feel at home. Those universal emblems that don't distinguish between us.

The continual moves in my early years of life prevented my becoming rooted to any one place or country. Even so, my sense of loss and confused identity were much more closely related to the discord and strains from those that were dear and near to me, than to the many breaks from my familiar surroundings and geographical bearings.

Hostility and division are at the opposite end of empathy and understanding

In my role as anaesthetist, I studied pain in its many varied forms and guises: its sources, the nervous networks that convey it across the body and up the spinal canal to be distributed to the various centres within the brain, its facilitation or suppression by particular events and circumstances, and the choice of devices and medicaments at our disposal to help alleviate and relieve it. In the course of my study and investigations I discovered that pain, whether it is triggered by physical injury or emotional grief – as different as these are – converges into a common pathway through that small, central, pea-like structure in the brain, the hypothalamus, leading to matching, measurable, physical reactions in our body. That all-important globule of brain tissue acts rather like a conductor of a vast orchestra, sending messages across a wide network of nerves and to every gland in the body that will, in turn, secrete the hormones that regulate the growth, repair and behaviour of every cell. The activated nerves and released hormones act in a complex, finely coordinated, symphonic-like whole to protect, compensate and recover our balanced and normal state. If the system is brought into play too much, too often, and too severely, some parts of it may at some stage start faltering and interfere with its elegant, beautifully equilibrated and carefully tuned, smooth running. Many of these changes have been quantified and ongoing research continues to throw light on these intricate and wondrous workings.

Those are the mechanisms; what is the experience?

Anger and ill will from someone trusted and deeply cared for can cut and churn deep into the quick. It punches a sickening sensation in the pit of the stomach, or sears our insides like a blade slicing and splicing through our entrails... Maybe the pain is the more intense when it isn't let out, but held back and turned inwards. Or, in other cases, its sharpness blunted and deadened by dissociating oneself from it. Such are its complexity and variations, subject to our psyche, as well as its physical aftermath.

On my return from the Antipodes to this part of the world, and in my search for answers, I revisited old neighbourhoods and surroundings from my early childhood, and met again friends and allies from that period of our lives, before our exile across two oceans. My mother came to Europe around the same time and we returned to those parts together as we retrieved those memories – which for me were vague and distant, while for her they were much closer, clearer and deeply affecting. Though we had come together for that journey into the past, she was fully absorbed in her moving reunions and exchanges with old friends, with whom she had shared so many difficult and anxious times together, and she was intent on catching up with all that had happened to them during those intervening years. I, on the other hand, kept on the margin as a silent observer, trying and barely starting to grasp the significance of it all.

I soon settled in London where I could practise medicine and embark on my postgraduate studies. Around this time, too, I met Kortokraks. He was visiting London to attend the wedding of one of his students in Westminster Abbey. He had just divorced his young wife in Germany, and his teaching in Salzburg, as Kokoschka's principal assistant at his *Schule des Sehens*, had ended with that institution's recent dissolution – though it would be restarted several years hence with him at its head.

I myself had just come back from a second trip to Deià, after my initial visit with my mother, when we had toured the villages and towns where we had once lived, and had had to leave, in France, Catalonia and Mallorca. On my more recent and leisurely visit, I had been struck and entranced by the island's honeyed, limpid light that shimmered in the air and burnished the silvered jade of the olive trees against the rust red earth and the stone houses of the town that blended into the mountainside. I had also been on my first trip to Greece, and visited some of the islands and become captivated by the dazzling white of the villages against the changing blues and turquoise of the sea and sky. In the port town of Mykonos, the varying shades of white on the houses, domed churches, steps and alleys had suddenly revealed a host of delicate colours – greens, violets, blues and pinks – within the white, to me. And I decided I needed to seize and recreate some of that magic my senses were waking up to and becoming so seduced by. I wished to learn to paint, while I continued to practice my medical skills for my living.

I had found my teacher in Kortokraks. His teaching was inspirational. A few honed words skilfully clarified how to concentrate on capturing the image, with all its light and shade, movement and flow, colour and life, onto paper. How to discard all preconceptions and expendable clutter that tend to obstruct our senses, and see it for what it is, not more not less, opening oneself up to take it in and absorb it in all its wonder and freshness. I set about practising it.

He, on the other hand, wanted to paint me. I seemed to fit into his vision of woman, or of someone he had always known, even before he set eyes on me. He had painted women who looked like me, long before we met. A stirring oil portrait he had produced back in 1947, when he was only nineteen, of a young Jewish girl in Germany – a great rarity at the time, when it was just beginning to recover from the Second World War – is often thought to be of our daughter Anna.

We found we had much in common, in both our backgrounds and our viewpoints. He had a deep understanding of the difficult and complex course of my life, and to me he represented much of what my mother had experienced in her youth that I was seeking and trying to comprehend. It was in-keeping with this pattern that we discovered that he had come across and befriended people when he was a young man in Germany, whom my mother and I had known, and I remembered visiting as a child, in Mexico. Gustav Regler, who had fought in Spain, and was known for his writing, was one. A woman called Nina, his mentor and friend in Paris in the 1950s, had known and assisted my mother in war-stricken Marseilles in 1940. Extraordinary coincidences. Or maybe simply a natural outcome of a background, along with a broad viewpoint and aspirations in common, in the context of the historical events that he and his parents, and my mother and I, had lived through. The beautiful and audacious Nina had also been part of Sartre's circle in the Café de Flore in Paris during the later years of the war, and Giacometti's model and mistress.

Kortokraks had also been a casualty of Hitler's war. His own childhood in a German Communist household – staunchly opposed to the growing new order of an exclusive, extreme, and alarming right wing nationalism – was put in jeopardy by the disagreements between his parents and the authorities when they objected to their son joining the Hitler Youth and taking part in the school's pro-Hitler curriculum. The young growing boy was interrogated by police, in an attempt to trick him into denouncing his parents and exposing their antifascist activities. Reaching further back to his early childhood, he had been frequently left on his own, frightened and lonely, while his parents attended meetings and distributed leaflets against the Nazis. He described to me how, on many of these occasions, he dragged himself dangerously across the tiled roof to climb through the window into his neighbour's home in search of company. They were living through harsh times and his father's photographic journalism didn't provide for their most basic needs. They had no electricity and used a kerosene lamp for lighting; Kortokraks recalled how, when the lamp ran out of fluid, they substituted it with the bicycle's carbide lamp. One night, when they returned home from the street demonstrations they had been taking part in, they found him fast asleep hugging the carbide lamp as another child would cuddle his teddy bear for warmth and comfort.

Some years later, when the war broke out, his mother took him to Austria and left him in the charge of a stranger, a woman who put him to work for her in her farm, and who appears to have treated him with little empathy. And towards the end of the war – when the German military were facing defeat and drafting fourteen- and fifteen-year-olds, the age he had reached – he witnessed shootings and hangings, by Nazi officers, of young friends who had not responded to their call to conscription, or in lieu of their brothers who could not be

Young Kortokraks in Worpswede

found. In the midst of all that disturbing, sinister confusion, the young Kortokraks had already decided he wanted to paint and started his art studies. His Austrian teacher helped him avoid enlisting in the army, which was fighting Hitler's last desperate stand, by employing him to record the artwork on traditional folk furniture – a service to the state, which waived conscription.

When armistice finally came, he walked, hitching the occasional ride, all the way back to his hometown, Ludwigshaven, on the Rhine. He returned to his art studies in Mannheim, and then went to live in the northern German town of Worpswede, renowned for its lively artistic community of which he became an active and integral part. Kortokraks had his first exhibition here, at the age of nineteen. His unusual talent was already recognised and clearly evident in his early works from his Worpswede years: portraits of other artists and writers he came to know there, and of the Northern German landscape around him. He was also working with a stage designer and created the sets for Stravinsky's *The Soldier's Tale*.

He came to live and decipher the world through his painting, putting into his canvasses all he observed and understood. He became intent on capturing not only the pictorial image, but the pulse and life and awe that form an integral part of it. His principal occupation and preoccupation were taken up with working out how to translate it from observation to finished work, whether it was a pretty girl, an inspiring landscape, or the latest atrocity committed in the world by some representative of humankind.

While other artists of our day might use modern technology and pay a team of assistants to wrap a vast landscape, or to stuff dead animals – a fitting statement of the market and celebrity based values of today's society – Kortokraks was instead putting all his heart and mind and rage, and long and arduously acquired painterly skills, to calculate how to juxtapose his paints on the canvas to express the human spirit and confusion and corruption, over and above his joyful renderings of the wonder of life in his vibrant landscapes, lush flowers and nubile women. Norbert Lynton, a distinguished art historian and critic of the time, expressed it more expertly when he wrote of his portraits "the act of painting them enshrines them and lifts them out of time and out of our space." And of their being "perceived beyond the paint..." indicating "a valuing of the subject, a feeling of awe even." In short, of Kortokraks's skill for catching, "not likeness... but *life*."

Our experiences in our histories and outlooks in common gave him a very real understanding of where I came from and what my life had been all about, and he made me feel dear and important to him, and I fitted his idea of what he liked to paint.

I also became aware of his formidably difficult and volatile character, as I watched him deliver his own brutal brand of rudeness when angry or crossed, or become meltingly engaging and gracious when he felt well disposed, whether to a tramp or a princess. And of these he had known several who had attended the Summer Academy in Salzburg, at the time when he was teaching under Kokoschka's directorship.

With time, I became caught under the spell of the notion that no sacrifice was great enough in the face of art. The kind of art that I respond to, which encapsulates our civilisation. Kortokraks's art expresses his celebration of nature, it draws on his penetrating insights evidenced in his portraits, and shows

Miriam and Kortokraks, after Rembrandt's *The Jewish Bride*

The Blind leading the Blind, after Bruegel

also humankind's less attractive attributes, as for instance in his studies, after Bruegel, of *The Massacre of the Innocents*, and his large powerful oil painting of *The Blind Leading the Blind*.

Not being rooted to a geographical bit of land, I was setting down my roots in the inspiration and meaning art gave me. The time-tested kind of art that expresses the values of the humane and universal.

But then...

After our life together, two daughters, and all we shared, I was also facing our growing discord from too great a disparity in our temperaments. He was wholly bent on his oeuvre to the callous disregard of everything else, including relationship and fatherhood, while I was spreading myself too thinly in my attempt to cope with the major demands at work and at home. I had long given up my own art work as, right from the start, there wouldn't have been room for more than one artist in the household, and it was all I could do to look after the practicalities of our every day. And – though I didn't give in easily – after twenty years of trying to find a way of living together, as I kept believing the answer must be there if only I could see it, the time had come to give in and bow out.

It was in my stubborn nature to attempt to understand what lay behind all things, big and small, that presented and unfolded before me, hoping to find a way within my capacity to solve them, whether it was a patient's illness or injury or suffering, or a situation in life. Kortokraks, on the other hand, threw all his energy and insights and everything he had into turning his observations about the world into his painting. He had no time or patience for give-and-take or compromise. His was a lonely occupation of which he bore the full brunt, while others around him were expected to fall in and assist him in his quest and his every need: collaboration – between spouses or friends or people – was a word he abhorred without apology. His anger and fury against everything that is wrong in the world would be turned against those closest to him, making life together stressful beyond whatever resolve or strength I had been intent on drawing on. And the hurt and the pain grew and welled up until they occupied the whole of me and were spilling over.

Miriam, during her marriage with Kortokraks

I have watched the rain patter against the window pane splattering it with copious water drops which, here and there, start spreading, touching and coalescing and then hedgingly, very slowly, begin drifting down, gather pace and finally form a fast narrow stream that plummets to the bottom. Like tears. So many tears. The rain may start pelting against the window more fiercely driving the tears to spill over into rivulets streaming down ever faster across the window pane. More and more of them. Proxy tears. From eyes that cry no more; that have lost the power to weep and remain dry and blank.

My mother used to sing me a song during our last years of the war in Marseilles,

> *Tengo tanto dolor,*
> *que no puedo llorar,*
> *yo quisiera llorar,*
> *y no tengo mas llanto...*

> I have so much pain,
> That I cannot weep,
> I would like to cry,
> But have no more tears.

Today the heavens are shedding so many tears. The raindrops streaming down the windowpane drive out the aching sorrow. They wash it all away allowing peace to shine through, as the sun breaks brightly through dark ominous clouds to warm and light the soul.

All the pain and grief in our marriage was captured in that one eye of the unfinished portrait. I can see it there – borne and fixed in that eye, and I the lighter for it. All the searing tension I carried deep inside me over those years has been lifted from me and moved into that eye on the canvas by Kortokraks, with his oil paints. As I stand before the unfinished portrait, I feel strangely liberated, absolved and disencumbered, free to fully engage and delight in my present and immediate surroundings, here and now.

Since we separated, Korotkraks sends me a bunch of red roses on my birthday and calls me on our wedding anniversary every year. He also shares with me all his important news. Most recently, I travelled with our two daughters to Salzburg to attend the premiere of a documentary on his life and work, which quoted him in the title *Ich Bin Einfach Noch Nicht Tot Genug*. I am simply not yet dead enough. And again for a retrospective exhibition of his work on his eighty-fifth birthday, along with the launch of a book on his artwork, which the Tate now keeps in its library and archives.

Further back in time, he had asked to read the draft of my autobiography, where I wrote about our life together. With some trepidation, I handed it over to him, and he took it to Italy where he was living, at the time, in his medieval tower in Tuscania. On his next visit to London, he came to see me in Duncan Terrace. His first words, with obvious relief in his voice, were, "It's not as bad as I thought," adding, "If anything, I feel closer to you now," and hugged me closely. Just as he had painted my portrait, I had written his, and he saw the depth of my recognition of him beyond our past battles and confrontations. And that mattered more.

The *recognition.*

Battles come and go, but the recognition, the valuing of the other, the understanding, in depth, beyond the more superficial quibbles and questions, is constant and enduring. What matters more.

That which I once experienced so powerfully with my mother. Kortokraks and my mother, though they too were in conflict with each other about everyday practicalities and behaviour, had both experienced Europe at war and all its attendant lessons and warnings and wisdom that grow from witnessing the extremes – both kindness and savagery in the face of overwhelming circumstances – in human nature and conduct. And they understood each other about the things that matter. Both were pivotal in my life, had caused me great hurt, a sense of betrayal even, maybe unintentionally I them too, and yet, beyond the hurt that fundamental valuing shone through. With Kortokraks, we recognised it in spite of our more superficial differences. With my mother, we had lost sight of it, and I was vainly trying to recover it.

My mother and I remained sadly distant from each other, over my adult, married and working life. Although we occasionally met when time allowed, the differences and misunderstandings that had sprung up in my later childhood and adolescence were not resolved.

Until a few hours before her death, when I was sitting by her bedside, close to her, and she whispered with great effort and difficulty in her weakened state,

"*I have understood.*"

She said little more after that. She died later that night.

Today I woke to a fine mist infused with the delicate blush of the early morning sun over sleepy London. It hung thickly over the Thames, obscuring the larger part of it and transforming the rest into a hazy ghostly trace of the river.

I remember the sunrises in Serifos. There, as night starts to give way to the faintest, first glimmer of light, I sometimes wake from my dreams and, still groggy from sleep, climb the stairs to let myself out onto the flat roof over my bedroom, and then still higher up onto the top roof-terrace, with the large square skylight, in the middle, over the living room. From here, I can barely make out the port and the mountains in the vague lifting darkness, while, further over towards the east, the sea stretches away under the vast pallid sky. I perch myself up by the white lacy chimney pot to get a better view, and watch the sun emerge smoothly and slowly from the sea – like a baby out of its womb – turning the Aegean into a sheet of shimmering gold. A vision going back to times long before humankind was here to witness and marvel at it, or to be overcome with awe at its sense of pristine renewal.

The experience of exile and survival can turn into a gift of life. Every moment to be cherished and lived to its fullest. And the world to be explored and experienced in its every shade and colour, its different traditions, outlooks and ways of life, music and dance, language and poetry. It is there to be learnt from, to cross boundaries and differences, to connect with one another, share our common traits and learn from our distinguishing customs. To open our eyes and take in the unknown. A large part of mankind, at different times in history, has had a great tradition of hospitality to the foreigner, making them feel welcome and at home. Its loss is anathema, a perversion...

But then, the world is, at the same time, a terrible and marvellous place. And our life on it too.

I have savoured a profusion of contrasting places, across the years, in the course of my life, on this earth. I have slept on a bed of pine needles under a starry sky in the King's Room of the crumbling ruins of a great Minoan palace poised over a tranquil green valley in Phaistos, Crete, and, some years later, surrounded by scented jasmine with my two small daughters in a veranda on the edge of the Chora on the Greek island of Paros, overlooked by a white monastery flooded in moonlight on the adjoining hillside. In Mykonos, just fresh from New Zealand, I roomed with a Greek family below the windmills of the white town overlooking the brilliant blue sea.

When I disembarked back in Europe from New Zealand, ready to launch into my new life in the continent of my birth, I slept in a room in a grand palazzo with high ceilings, marble floors and antique rococo furniture overlooking the River Arno in Florence, and, in Paris, in a small hotel near La Madeleine in a saggy bed with a roll pillow and wine-red cover from where I gazed at the irregular scape of the French roofs and chimneys through the window.

In the city of Nuremberg, I stood on the same spot in its massive stadium, now echoing in its vast emptiness, where Hitler once barked hysterically at a packed crowd stretched at his feet like a swelling sea thundering with one voice "Heil!", right arms flicked forward in one synchronised movement, as a single gigantic organism, in an astonishing reflex mass response to one small moustachioed man.

Berlin – the charred remains of the Kaiser Wilhelm Memorial Church's bell tower starkly silhouetted like a burnt limb stump piercing the sky, elegant display cases and affluent shop fronts along the Kurfürstendamm and, a few streets on, the neglected crumbling walls and rubble from the final bombing by the allies scattered all over near The Wall.

Copenhagen, Oslo, Stockholm. Sweden's pine forests flushed pale pink in the northern light; rivers covered with logs floating to their destinations; pretty lakeside cottages with masses of bright flowers. Midsummer celebrations on the banks of a large lake under the light, starry sky, and the beautiful young man who left his group of friends to pick me out and whirl me away laughing and dancing on the grass asking me so many questions while his pretty girlfriend was trying to retrieve him. In Norway, the roofs of peasants' cottages covered with tall grass, the odd tree or shrub, and a goat munching the turf up there. Close to the Arctic Circle: the midnight sun softly radiantly grazing a cool horizon to start rising again as I watched from a hill on the Lofoten island nearest the mainland.

New York, the Chelsea Hotel lobby crammed with a disparate sample of art objects, naturalistic to abstract, traditional to outrageous, brash, grandiose and strange, paintings, sculptures and other sundry items as clients' payment for their rooms and penthouse flats. We shared the lift with pop-stars, actors, singers and musicians from jazz to classical, and other characters, fringe, famous and in-between, lavishly dressed, bejewelled and perfumed, brightly coloured manes, Mohican haircuts, or elegant tailored suits.

The Gran Hotel – my father's favourite in Mérida, Mexico

– with its tiled courtyard, palm trees and benches and lively-eyed boys waiting to shine your shoes, several storeys of old Spanish colonial charm facing a leafy square, its cool restaurant lined with busy tables in starched white tablecloths and tasty local dishes like *pollo pibil*, everything fresh, clean and well kept when my father took me to the Maya pyramids in Chichen Itza on my visit to Mexico after New Zealand, yet the same hotel sadly neglected, greying paint flaking off its walls in Mérida's damp heat, on my last visit with him when he too had aged and was becoming infirm and asking to share his room with me, feeling uncharacteristically vulnerable and afraid to be alone, seeking to rely on me should he need help. From his now grown daughter, whom he overlooked when she was small and in need of help, along with her mother...

A wooden bungalow with a revolving fan above the bed to cool the room in the moist tropical heat, in the hotel's extensive grounds with a parrot, two spider monkeys, a forest of bamboo and a vast natural swimming pool crisscrossed with boulders next to impenetrable jungle near the ancient Maya city of Palenque, with its pyramids, Maya stone figures, relief sculpture and small museum – with my daughter Anna. In San Cristobal de las Casas, a large room and tiny en-suite bathroom with colourful hand-painted flowers on tiles and basins in a Spanish colonial hotel with a garden dotted with benches, a blue and white tiled fountain and the small group of Maya women with long black plaits, thick woollen skirts and their handmade wares around the entrance.

I have slept wrapped in my sleeping bag on hard icy ground inside a pup tent in a clearing of New Zealand's lush native bush, and on a slab of rock in thick drizzle when night came while climbing mountains in Otago. I visited a hotel in a cave in Matmata in the Tunisian desert, and stayed in the Jade Screen Tower Hotel on top of a high mountain facing the Heavenly Capital Peak in Huangshan.

The endless variety and alternative combinations of life, their cultures, histories and viewpoints, which broaden perspectives, and put one's own into context.

My academic medical work also gave me the opportunity to see more of the world. In Manila, where I was attending an International Congress of Anaesthesiology, I listened to Imelda Marcos's opening speech, in the vast conference hall facing the sea, in which she was at pains to find common ground between the life saving and pain relieving functions of anaesthesia and what she was doing to her country and her people. Breaking my route back to London in Bangkok, my hotel room's wall to wall panoramic view of the river and its busy traffic of barges, skiffs, ships, canoes and ferries, with the colonial Oriental Hotel downriver where I watched a tradition-al Thai wedding reception. One river-bus stop across the river, I would dine in the large open air restaurant and tried to cool my tongue between mouthfuls of chilli and lemongrass prawn salad to the background of the plaintive sounds of Thai music, while I watched the life of the river float by.

And when I started translating an Andean Argentine author's works I discovered following a lecturing visit to Buenos Aires, I visited the vast empty plains at the foot of the Cordillera where the air is thin, the sun burning hot, the shade icy cold, and the silence so strong that it makes your ears buzz. This place has remained so isolated across the centuries that the people still speak an antiquated Spanish left over from the Conquistadors mixed with a smattering of local indigenous Quechua and Aymara words: a fascinating challenge when I set out to translate the author Héctor Tizón's literary works.

The centuries-old students' quarters, smelling of old wood and books, in St Catherine's College in Cambridge, when participating at an obstetric anaesthetists' conference. The neat, box-like, modern rooms overlooking the undulating green lawns and leafy countryside around Stirling University in Scotland, with cocktails in the local castle preceding the Anaesthetic Association Meeting. And in Edinburgh University, the triumphant procession in kilts to the tune of bagpipes when the haggis was brought into the banqueting hall on the last day of that conference. The farmhouse on the western coast of the Scottish island of Arran, its heather covered hills a feast of amber and lavender tones, where I stayed with three other female anaesthetists from the Royal London Hospital after the meeting in Stirling, to wake in the morning to a Scottish breakfast of porridge and a plateful of fried eggs, kippers, sausages, mushrooms and tomatoes topped with tea and toast while facing the farm's animal menagerie from our table by the window in the porch.

I had been separated from Kortokraks for several years, and was picking up my life again. I was moving forward with my academic work at the Royal London Hospital, and my clinical work and teaching in the labour ward at Newham Hospital. At home my two daughters were nearing their mid and late teens.

Around this time I was offered a chance to form part of a delegation of European anaesthetists to visit China, to exchange notes with our Chinese counterparts.

Our hosts in Beijing took us to the Hospital of Traditional Chinese Medicine where we saw the enormous hall with wall to wall shelves and drawers labelled with medicinal herbs and animal parts for the preparation of patients' medicines from dried scorpions, chunks of snakes, mammalian endocrine glands, and countless other specimens from the vegetable and animal kingdom, all carefully labelled and stored in the lined wooden drawers. Through a large door at the end of that room, the vast kitchen where each prescription was being weighed, mixed and prepared in the long rows of boiling cauldrons, the whole room enveloped in mist from their vapour. In other hospitals we saw the growing, still fledgling, western pharmacy and methods practiced alongside and in combination with their traditional methods, acupuncture, herbal and animal medicines and modern drugs used together to treat each patient's medical conditions – the western arguments and separation of the two systems totally absent here.

We learnt too of the stark difference in attitudes to pain: acupuncture used not so much for pain relief or anaesthesia but for treating medical conditions in all the hospitals we visited. Pain relief was not a concern that our Chinese anaesthetic colleagues thought about. In the many operating theatres we visited, we were shown difficult, sometimes heroic operations on wide awake, uncomplaining patients under epidural or local nerve blocks only partially effective. An important consideration in China was the economy of this form of anaesthesia, in preference to the West's expensive machines, drugs and equipment. Patients of all ages, even small children, lay completely still, the pain from the procedure borne stoically and unflinchingly, with not so much as a squeeze of their hand or a whisper of encouragement from the staff. We asked about pain clinics in one of the more comprehensive and advanced hospitals we visited in Shanghai, and our hosts looked baffled at the idea.

It was clear how, what we take for granted, accept as a given right, without question, in one culture, may be completely absent from the way of thinking in another.

We were treated by our Chinese hosts to lavish banquets with such delicacies as jellyfish tentacles, hundred-year-old eggs, ducks' feet, starfish and sea cucumbers. We spent a day exploring the vast complex of the Forbidden City, where elaborately worked turquoise and blue ceramic façades stretch above austere rectangular buildings with wooden lattice windows and tiled roofs ending in upturned eaves bearing rows of curious mythical figures. We visited the Summer Palace of past emperors with its great lake, tall pagodas, long roofed-in colonnades with delicately painted scenes of everyday life during the Qing Dynasty illustrating their history, stone courtyards and moon gates. We saw the Ming tombs, and walked on a strip of the Great Wall, awe-inspiring in its construction and its stunning views.

And before me, a tiny chink of a different world and people was opening out. Where the austere went side by side with the intricately ornate, and rigid conformity with original insight. A people who once named its vast country, which was virtually isolated from the rest of the world by the sea along its eastern border, the desert in the north, and the highest mountain ranges in the south and west, Tianxia, or All Under Heaven; a people who had described in the medical text of their ancient tome, *The Yellow Emperor's Manual*, the presence in the body of a complex system of air and liquid channels to produce our life energy, long before William Harvey's discovery of the circulation; and whose advanced and sophisticated medical knowledge – until overtaken by the West's scientific method, in which controlled investigation replaced empiricism and tradition – was described by one of their own sages as "a mixture of pearls and rubbish".

The Beijing Hotel where we stayed was a large rambling complex in the main street leading to Tiananmen Square, made up of the old, Chinese section, a more recent area with a Russian flavour and influence, and the modern section. There was an air of relaxed, jaded elegance along its maze of sombre halls, waiting rooms and restaurants, where every face seemed to have an interesting story behind it: a seasoned traveller, maybe a writer or journalist, or a businessman or other professional bent on some challenging project in China.

In Nanjing, our next stop, the whole town was covered with Chinese cabbages, spread out on the ground along street pavements, porches and doorways, strung across windowsills and hanging from balconies, Chinese cabbages everywhere we looked, to dry for the winter months. Unlike the Beijing Hotel, the modern international skyscraper where we were lodged in Nanjing towered high above the rest of the old, low storey buildings of the city.

Shanghai, our third and final stop, was a stepping-stone to our more familiar world with its old charm and Western undertones. We sat around a large round table in the hotel restaurant enjoying our last meals together, thirteen anaesthetists in all, from Denmark, Iceland, France, Holland, Germany and

England, feasting on a sumptuous Chinese spread closer in kind to that served in the West.

Layer upon layer of dark mountain peaks pierce the pale eastern sky as it turns every moment lighter and brighter, while fleecy clouds drift and streak across it, turning from delicate pink through coral and crimson into fiery scarlet. The soot-black, knotted fingers of two ancient pines on a rocky promontory stand out against the smudgy outline of distant wooded mountains, while the first twitters of distant birds tune up. And then a sudden hush, a breath-holding stillness, descends across the whole scene, as a wild speck of brilliant gold makes its appearance on the horizon. As it grows, the dawn's spectral light turns into the honeyed blush of early morning. The sparkling burning dot becomes a sliver, and the sliver the greater part of a circle, until a ball of liquid fire detaches itself from the mountain and dances into the pristine sky, free at last. The masses of Chinese who have also risen early and been waiting on the mountain for this moment with an incessant loud chatter, now start busily organising themselves with their cameras to take each other's photographs against the rising sun on these sacred mountains of Huangshan, where their Buddhist forebears have come to pay homage – as the gigantic Chinese characters etched into the rock-face in various sites bear witness – and watch the sunrise, hopefully in more silent and solemn contemplation, for thousands of years.

I had returned to China with Rachel, my classmate and friend in medical school. In the short intervening years, gone were the blue Mao suits which had been worn everywhere by man and woman alike on my previous trip, to be replaced by the men's now baggy Western trousers and women's colourful dresses and bright makeup. Strictly regulated business, any breach of which had been severely punished, sometimes by execution, had given way to what looked like a free-for-all, free enterprise encouraged by the authorities. All of which, flashed forward to the present, has progressed exponentially to a growing group of entrepreneur socialist billionaires and the ultra fashionable who have caught up with, and in many spheres even overtaken, the West. The China of today, poised to lead the world...

Many of the changes I found in the short intervening years between my first and second visit were fairly radical – yet they did not seem to ripple the underlying central communist power and control over the populace. The international hotels, inside which no Chinese, not even our medical hosts, had been allowed to set foot on my first visit, were now patronised by the increasing number of wealthy Chinese. And we had a free choice of where to stay, even from among the more modest hotels aimed at the local population, which would have been strictly banned to any foreigner on my previous trip to China. The Dao and Buddhist temples, with their gigantic, painted wooden figures and braziers of burning candles, empty on my last visit, were now teaming with worshipping Chinese.

We travelled with the Chinese in trains and buses and visited ancient towns once admired by Marco Polo. We saw Suzhou, a traditional centre of silk making and enchanting gardens with a brash, modern principal street, though the old life bustling with markets and lively scenes was still going on around the canals and in the side streets lined with plane trees; Yangzhou, an ancient centre of art and more, formally designed, traditional gardens; and then on, from Tunxi and Huangshan, to the beautiful city of Hangzhou, where we watched from a rowboat on its West Lake an immense, blood-red sun slowly close in on and sink into its waters, leaving a wide streak of red gold in its wake, the fishermen on the neighbouring boats silhouetted against it.

I sat at an intricately carved antique Chinese desk making a note of my impressions in the suite I was sharing with Rachel. We had installed ourselves in these quarters on raised ground behind the main hotel. From where I sat I looked down on the river, far below, which skirts around the old town of Tunxi, with willowy men and women wading in up to their calves to beat their washing. To my right, I looked through a latticed wooden divide into our Chinese living room and the forest of bamboo beyond. Tunxi, with its ancient, thousand year old street from the Song Dynasty that transports one back into another world and age, is the nearest centre to Huangshan – those mountains in ancient Chinese drawings enveloped in mist, with pines growing out at odd angles from their craggy peaks – which we had come to see. In Huangshan, we followed trails up the steep steps cut into the rock, past blazing, autumnal splashes of coppery red and orange breaking out of greener vegetation or on a sloping smooth expanse of rock, and past famous landmarks of ancient pines and odd rock formations sought and venerated by Chinese monks and travellers since ancient times. Moving among the throng of Chinese visitors climbing with us were young boys with fast, leaden gait, balancing baskets, heavy with cement and other construction materials or victuals for the hotels at the top, from the ends of the bamboo sticks strung across their wiry shoulders. Now and then a pair of them were struggling in tandem under the weight of a fat Chinese, maybe from Taiwan or Hong Kong, reclining lazily under his hat on a wicker chair balanced on top of the sticks strung across their young carriers. We met two students from Shanghai and walked part of the way with them, exchanging ideas and information. They explained to us that in Russia, first the political system was changed, to be followed by the introduction of western concepts and practices, while in China this order was reversed, to maintain order instead of the confusion, chaos and criminal elements that had been let loose in Russia.

A few months later I was sitting in the snack bar of the Washington Hyatt, on the evening of my arrival in Washington to attend the World Congress of Anesthesiologists. The tall, young, Chinese waiter who was serving me spoke American with an American accent and was friendly, informal and assertive, resting his hand on the back of my shoulder when speaking to me, the way an American might, but no Chinese in China. He had Chinese features and American expressions and movements. And, in that waiter, I suddenly saw three millennia of ingrained culture and tradition, of Chinese 'roots', vanished in one generation.

That waiter epitomised for me the relativity of cultural and national identity: remove the accumulated layers acquired from our surroundings and experiences, and we have a human being. There is no such thing as "purity of race", or of culture, nationality, or religion: all the harm done in the world in the name of our differences is, in essence, absurd.

My room on the Hyatt's fifth floor overlooked the hotel's

inner court with a white lake, in the middle of which was a kidney-shaped white island with a white grand piano and a pianist in a white suit, white shoes and white bow tie plucking Chopin's trills and arpeggios that floated up the hotel well into my room, late into the night, even through the closed window.

From a straw mattress on the stone floor in Casablanca to the Washington Hyatt. From enforced exile to a celebration of diversity...

A spectrum of impressions plucking through diverse lands, traditions, years and circumstances. Observing and savouring sensations that cut across lifestyles, latitudes and continents; in mountains, near lakes, and by the sea; loud, busy, modern cities and tranquil, remote places with nature still intact.

As I endeavour to create a portrait of my mother, brush stroke by brush stroke, a woman begins to emerge whose life was deeply affected and fashioned by major events in twentieth century Europe and used her strength and foresight to overcome the huge challenges that faced her. Someone who drew many admirers, starting from her youth and across her life, who lived assiduously and was passionate in her convictions and her loves, but who must have also gone through times of overwhelming uncertainty and despair that she kept close to her chest and wouldn't admit or disclose.

Three other, quite different women, crossed my path, fleetingly and by chance.

I am driving in our old Renault 4 along the western coast road of the Greek island of Corfu, with Kortokraks in the seat next to me and our two small daughters Rebekah and Anna in the back of the car, surrounded by the Mediterranean countryside. Not another soul or house in sight.

We suddenly come upon a woman picking figs by the side of the road; she is collecting them in the pouch of her upturned long skirt and then emptying them into her basket. She is very thin, wrinkled and weather-beaten, I think maybe she is a hundred years old, yet she stands tall and erect. I stop alongside her. She walks up to the car and picks some of her figs from the pouch and offers them to us. I ask if she wants a lift. I show her the seat next to me, and point in turn at her and back at the seat, until she understands. A huge grin transforms her ancient crinkled face and she gathers her basket full of figs, straightens out her skirt over her crumpled, thick brown stockings and her shoes worn to shreds with walking and age, and, after Kortokraks has moved to the back with the girls, she climbs into the seat next to me and sits down like a queen, her grin of immense delight still fixed on her face. It is clear she has never seen the inside of a car before and she is enjoying the experience. Some eight or nine kilometres further on, we enter a small village. She sits up very straight, and becomes delightedly self-conscious. As the battered Renault 4 starts driving through the central and actually only street, all the youngsters begin to gather around the car followed by the older people in the village, calling out in glee and full of surprise. They finally indicate a house where I am to stop. A whole family comes out of the house expressing amazement and bursting into wild amused laughter and, all the while exclaiming excitedly, give way to her as she steps out of the car, tall and proud and still smiling like a child with a new toy. The family insists we come in and make a big fuss around us, offering us fruit and drinks and animatedly pointing her out in old family photographs, before they finally allow us to go on our way.

Rachel and I climb on an old bus in Tunxi on our way to Shaoxin County, a small nearby town. At the next stop, a young local girl steps on the bus. She is tall, slim, long-limbed, and outstandingly beautiful with high, broad cheekbones, large, doe-like, Asian eyes, an olive complexion, and her hair careful-ly waved and woven into an elaborate style framing her stun-ning face. Any model scout would snap her up, I think to myself, and I can see her on the cover of *Vogue*. She wears a burgundy red velvet dress, mid-calf length, of a shapely and attractive design, but cheap synthetic material, stretched over her bulging pregnant stomach. She is carrying a small suitcase that has seen better days, and she sits down on the side bench facing the doorless entrance area in the middle of the bus, suit-case by her side, her face sulky and sad - a kind of cold, stony, resigned look which is at odds with her beauty and her preg-nancy. I wonder: what might her story be? Was she thrown out by a wealthy old lover when she became pregnant and was of no more use to him? After a few moments, while I am still in my reverie trying to imagine her life and history, she suddenly stands up, leans her graceful figure forward towards the open entrance of the bus, clears her throat stridently to round up her spit and ejects it with an experienced precision from the moving bus out into the street. With that unexpected gesture, the doors snap shut on the mystery, and I realise simply that I shall not penetrate it.

A short while later, as we walk through the streets of

Shaoxin County exploring the small ancient town, which appears never to have had a tourist before inside it, a watchmaker sitting in a doorway lifts his gaze momentarily from his absorbing work and, encountering the small, fair, round-eyed, image of Rachel, his eyes peel back in terror as though he is seeing an apparition from outer space.

We are the strange ones, the unfamiliar, here.

I have come to Avignon to give a talk at an international meeting on literature, exile and identity, and I am staying, with my friends, Angela and Jonathan – who have come from Athens to attend the meeting – in a hotel in a street off the leafy central square, Place de l'Horloge, with Avignon's town hall, Hotel de Ville. I know Angela from New Zealand where she was the daughter of my professor of anatomy at my medical school in Dunedin, and Jonathan teaches English language and literature at the Athens College, where Angela also works. As we return to the hotel, late one evening, my attention is caught by a vague shape in the darkness lying on the cobbled pavement facing the hotel entrance. I cross over to see what it is and it sharpens into a crumpled black heap with a garment thrown over it loosely outlining angled bony limbs and, on the middle of it, a black hat pulled down over what I now see is the slumped figure of a woman completely hidden underneath. She is slouched on top of a bulging, dark blue suitcase against a lamppost, a few steps from Avignon's central square with its brightly lit Hotel de Ville. I cannot detect even the most minimal movement in that heap. I wonder if she is breathing. Is she alive? "No, she's not on drugs," the hotel receptionist says as we enter and I ask about her. "She's always there.

129

Refuses any help. She's been like that since she lost her family. People say they were all killed outright except for one surviving daughter who comes every now and then to give her something to eat, or change her clothes. In a car crash or something. She studied philosophy at the university. Used to be a teacher. And she owns a large beautiful house somewhere out in the country." The next day she is sitting on the steps of the Hotel de Ville with her suitcase. She lifts her face this time. It is devoid of expression, grey and shockingly old, on her young, thin, wasting body.

A small mosaic of life on this earth. Of which we all form part.

Kortokraks, in front of his self portrait, at the private view of his exhibion at the
Wolfgang Gurlitt Gallery, Munich, 1964

The Colour of Life

Billowing white clouds, bright and luminous, float alongside a heavy, sombre, rain-loaded mass looming over the mountain range facing my terrace, in Serifos. The cloud formations are continually shifting position and changing shape with the strong blustery winds sweeping across the island and the Aegean skies. Further over, beyond the port, over the sea and towards the horizon, a vaporous mantle of mist turns darker and denser as it blends seamlessly into the long low form of the island of Milos, which in turn merges imperceptibly into the smoother bluer sea, shading off from one to the other like a smudgy gouache.

The weather is subject to very abrupt changes in the Aegean. I have seen a thick fog suddenly descend and fill the valley and blanket the port, obliging an approaching ferry to stop in its tracks and blow its horn as it is suddenly and unexpectedly cut off and turns invisible.

Back in London, I have seen through my living room window a brilliant shaft of light from the lowering sun burn a blinding silver mirror onto the river Thames through a murky mist. On another day, a thick black carpet of cloud obscured one half of the sky while the other was bright blue, sunny and clear.

Today the sun shines down on the river from a pristine blue sky over the whole of London. It is Sunday, and a flotilla of small, one-man canoes has emerged from under the railway bridge beyond St Mary's Church, and has stopped for a short break next to one of the residential barges under my window. They are a visual feast, flaunting every colour of the rainbow – red, yellow, orange, violet, green and blue – as they gather together, stop paddling and remain in one spot gently bouncing on the water. One is fuchsia pink, even. Their paddles are brightly coloured too, each in a different tint from its canoe, and the paddlers, men and women of all ages, are wearing caps and windbreakers of bold and more contrasting colours. It is a lively spectacle on what is commonly a uniformly grey-toned river.

I have seen a river scene with boats painted by André Derain with the strong colours of his Fauve style, producing a similar effect. The orange, green, red and blue wooden rowing boats moored close to the green grassy riverbank stand out against the light glistening surface of the river Seine at Chatou, where the Fauves and many of the Impressionists liked to paint. There are river views with colourful boats on that same stretch of the Seine by Vlaminck and Renoir, and in Monet's river scenes the reflections of the boats and the sky ripple and sparkle, along with his carefully placed and judged brushstrokes of myriad colours that create the water.

The intense celebration of colour, form, texture and movement by these painters was overturning the more formal and structured traditions in art that had ruled the previous centuries. And it, in turn, was giving way to yet other art forms, which were growing out of the political and ideological battles that started convulsing the world and would shortly lead to two world wars.

As the nineteenth century turned to the twentieth, writers, artists and thinkers from all over Europe, as well as from the

American continent, were converging on Paris to join and learn from and exchange ideas with the buoyant, fertile, and radically changing art and literary world in the French capital, where all these activities were concentrated, fermenting and taking shape. André Breton was setting down the philosophical foundations of the Surrealist movement, rooted in its fervent opposition and protest against the established order, in concert with the new Marxist and anarchist ideologies that were intent on overthrowing that order, considered no longer tenable or endurable. In the heated discussions of the times, this emerging art form – with its precedents in the art of Dante and Hieronymus Bosch, among others – has been described as creative acts of revolt realised through unleashing the unconscious and freeing the imagination, with the aim to confront, provoke, shock and challenge society. André Breton wrote, "It was in the black mirror of anarchism that surrealism first recognised itself."

On a recent visit to Nicole Milhaud at her Bateau Lavoir studio in Paris, I stopped in my tracks in the Place Émile Goudeau, under the shade of the thick foliage from the square's ancient trees, as I was walking across it on my way to Nicole's. As I surveyed my enchanting surroundings, I found myself turning back the years and trying to visualise the young, slight, impoverished, little-known Pablo Ruiz Blasco – soon to settle for his mother's name Picasso – crossing this very space and ground. He is wrapped in his woollen scarf and dark jacket over his slim-fit twill trousers – jeans had not yet taken over – as an ancient photograph shows him, at the bottom of this square. To be followed by other friends and fellow artists he was exchanging ideas and working alongside with: the young Georges Braque – whom my father mentioned meeting, in his Paris years, before he rose to fame – Modigliani, Van Gogh, Gauguin, Derain, and so many more. The writers Apollinaire and Cocteau also frequented Le Bateau Lavoir and crossed this space, not to forget the legendary Gertrude Stein, whose company Hubert and Seppl would join, when they settled in Paris, in years to come. They had all walked through this square on their way to their lodgings and studios at Le Bateau Lavoir, or simply to meet and talk and argue and discuss and try out their ideas, which were so novel and original and, to much of the outside world, outrageous and unworkable, and yet would grow and become fully accepted and established some years on.

Flash further back, and Le Bateau Lavoir's ramshackle wooden building overlooking this square is an anarchists' den, and before that a furrier's warehouse, which had taken over from what had been a piano factory. Flying still further back through time, and it is a guinguette where people are eating and drinking, playing music and dancing, around a huge old pear tree in the middle of the square, which forms the guinguette's garden. A group of them sit around a table on a platform built into the branches of the tree, chattering and enjoying their drinks and meals amongst its foliage. The guinguette is named quite appropriately *Le Poirer Sans Pareil* ... The Pear Tree Without Equal.

I drag my attention back to the present, and I am standing on this same cobblestoned square now scattered with park benches and covered with shady trees, its outdoor café at its lower corner filled with today's people sitting around their tables in cheerful, twenty-first century, chat.

I pick up again where I left off on my way to Nicole. I have come to Paris to attend the vernissage of Theys's sculpture and paintings and celebrate his life. Nicole's tiny spare room under the glass roof is taken up by visiting relatives this time, and her neighbour, Georgiana Colvile, has invited me to stay at her apartment a few doors along from Le Bateau Lavoir's studio complex. Georgiana's lower ground flat, in what looks from the street like an unremarkable house half-way up Montmartre, occupies a beautiful, brightly lit space full of books and paintings and colourful curios and mementoes she has collected from all over the world. Her plate glass windows, which stretch across the length of her flat, face the trees and vegetation at the back of the house and look steeply down onto a cascade of green leafy terraces ending below in the Bateau Lavoir's lower floors, now turned into a large gallery where Theys's work is showing.

Kortokraks has also been invited by Nicole to Theys's exhibition. He came from Salzburg and is staying at his usual Hôtel Du Quai Voltaire, facing the Seine, close to the Louvre, which he likes to share with its famous, past guests: Oscar Wilde, Hemingway, Pissarro, Wagner, Baudelaire, among others. He telephoned me and suggested we meet and have lunch at the Musée d'Orsay. For all our previous stormy relations, both during our 20 years together and another 20 or more separated by now, on this occasion we had a pleasant and relaxed time together at the museum's grand restaurant, sitting under the high painted ceiling and huge crystal chandeliers. After lunch, he suggested I go and look at some of the museum's art collections, while he sat in the main hall and waited for me, he

Kortokraks on his last trip to Paris

being already familiar with the artworks and finding walking difficult, with his advanced heart condition. The once strong, athletically built, good-looking man had shrunk into himself, now much reduced in stature: a small, bent, hollow cage, who walked slowly on his painful legs, with a stick. But when he spoke, he summoned and poured all his strength into his firm, deep, unwavering voice to declare his ever, uncompromising stance and convictions.

Kortokraks's own retrospective exhibition had taken place the previous month, at Salzburg's Mirabell Schloss gardens' pavilion. It had displayed his large, political, "rage" paintings, mostly made up of mixed media pastiches and collages, which gave vent to his horror at particular atrocities and, more generally, at much of what was going on in the world. It was launched with a glowing, laudatory speech by the Salzburg state's visual arts representative. Kortokraks, much moved, in his frail, bent frame, sat down in front of the large gathering, with a sheaf of papers bearing a speech he had prepared for the occasion. As the sheets of papers kept flying about, he ended up by just talking to the audience. The main content of his speech was to acknowledge that through all his years of hardship and struggles to maintain his artistic integrity against all odds in today's art market and fashions, the one person who had always stood by him, supported him, and not let him down, he said – to my astonishment, as this was not something I had ever heard from him before – was his wife.

As unwell as he was, he would be propelled to keep going by his sheer, monumental determination. His stubborn will to keep painting was all he had left to overcome his physical infirmity. He had called me in London on our anniversary, as was his want, with "Do you know what day it is today?" Adding, "Next year we'll have a huge fireworks display." I tried to think why. "It will be our fiftieth..."

He died just short of a month later.

I had a final look at him before the coffin lid was closed and he was lowered into the ground. His cheeks cold and pale, his face – which had always been so expressive, whether in gentle empathy or close observation, in angry disagreement or haughty disapproval, and every other shade of emotion – now blank. He still had the small tuft of hair, in the middle, above his forehead, that wouldn't be tamed and wouldn't allow me to brush it down with my hand: symbol maybe of his will over mine, even now... His right eye was closed in repose, but his left was slightly open, the colour of green sea. I tried to close it, but it refused, as though it had not finished looking at the world and needed to go on seeing forever, in keeping with his painting passion in life. I lightly kissed his cold, bloodless cheek for the last time, and the coffin was closed.

I thought of him in the dark, and of course: his eye didn't see anymore, it was glazed and still, it had lost the fervour of looking, its intelligence, its sparkle. It had left its vision elsewhere. It was to be found in all his works he had left behind – one only had to look at them to find him, very much alive, and for all his passion for life, luminous insights and deep convictions, there to be shared.

After he had been lowered into the earth under a maple tree, overlooked by the mountains he loved to paint, the sun shone softly and the day was crisp and clear and the light pure, and his presence appeared to be permeating the landscape he had so often captured in his artwork.

He had acquired a large number of devoted admirers in and around Salzburg. The bank manager in a historical town in the mountains south of Salzburg, whose bank is hung in every room with Kortokraks artworks, described to me how he had driven him to a particular spot where he wanted to draw the landscape, and how he caused a traffic jam in that remote mountain road. The bank manager had helped him out of the car, and Kortokraks had moved very slowly, step by step, leaning against his hand-carved stick, as he crossed the road. Some workers who were repairing the road that day, cleared it from their machines for him, and were holding up the mounting queue of traffic, in the narrow twisting mountain road, to let him pass, until he reached the bench on the other side of the road and sat down and positioned himself. Holding the drawing paper on the board, and with his broken, heavily-used colour pastels – cobalt blue, magenta pink, sulphur yellow, carmine red, ochre brown and indeed the whole box-full – next to him on the bench, he immersed himself into the snow peaked mountains, the woods and the changing sky in front of him, which he had chosen to draw, with his full concentration, eyes squeezed into slits moving from landscape to paper and back again. The pastel landscape, in a beautiful gold-leaf frame, now hangs in the bank manager's office.

Nicole called me a month later to tell me that Daniel – her first husband and the son of Darius Milhaud, who had been co-assistant at Kokoschka's school along with Kortokraks, the two having formed a firm friendship at the time – had just died in Pietrasanta, his northern Italian studio home close to Carrara, from where he used the marble for his sculptures. The two men, who had shared one of their most important periods in their early life dedicated to their art, had both died within four weeks of each other. Though Nicole and Daniel had been divorced many years already, as Kortokraks and I had also been separated, their deaths brought home many deeply moving and conflicting memories. As deaths do.

The exhibition Nicole was holding of her second husband, Theys, at which Kortokraks and I had one of our last, most peaceful and amicable meetings, had been in commemoration of Theys, who had also died two years earlier.

Georgiana returned from the south of France where she had been staying, while she loaned me her beautiful Parisian flat on the occasion of Theys's exhibition. I stayed on another night, before returning to London, to exchange news with Georgiana over dinner. She is a specialist in the women surrealist painters of the twentieth century, and she was astonished to discover that I knew Alice Rahon, whom she has researched and written about. I told her how, when I was a child in Mexico, we used to visit her home next to Frida Kahlo's and not far from Trotsky's — who had been assassinated shortly before we arrived in the country — all of whom formed part of Alice's circle: their art and politics and ideologies being closely inter-twined and constantly re-examined. And, sometimes, creating violent confrontations and disagreements.

Alice and her surrealist painter husband Wolfgang Paalen were part of that large flood of refugees leaving Paris and other parts of France and Europe in the lead up to and in the early years of the Second World War, many of them on the same ship my mother and I boarded in Casablanca, in November, 1941. The timing had become critical, as Hitler's war was, at that stage, turning every moment more ruthless and relentless in the pursuit of its sinister objectives and his supremacy.

My mother and I formed part of that large shipload of passengers on the Portuguese vessel, the Serpa Pinto, on its journey to Mexico, to escape from the persecution in Europe of Jews, political dissidents, artists, intellectuals, ex-patriate and stateless "undesirables".

An archival document lists those passengers in the Serpa Pinto who, on their arrival in Mexico, were offered assistance to start them off in their new lives. Their "original" nationali-ties — many of the passengers having had these annulled and

SS Serpa Pinto

become stateless – were reported as being from France, Germany, Belgium, Holland, Poland, Czechoslovakia, Austria, Hungary, Russia, Italy, Spain, Turkey and one from Brazil. Their religions are disclosed as Jewish, Catholic, Protestant and some, whose names would suggest otherwise, described their religion simply as "Not Jewish". Their professions included journalists, writers, historians, professors, linguists, printers, photographers, film producers, theatre performers, composers, lawyers, doctors, psychiatrists, pharmacists, nurses, teachers, businessmen, a mayor and a pilot.

In addition to my mother's and my names in this list, I came across Robert Capa's assistant and future husband of Leonora Carrington, Emeric Weisz, and the French poet and partner of the surrealist artist Remedios Varo, Benjamin Péret, among others I recognised and whom I remember as friends in our years in Mexico. We journeyed together across the Atlantic on the Serpa Pinto for several weeks, my mother cementing new friendships and connections as she shared in common with many of the passengers their history of standing against Franco in Spain and other antifascist activities, till we arrived in the Mexican port of Veracruz.

Senya and Mollie had been passengers on the Serpa Pinto.

In our first years in Mexico, I remember our frequent visits to them, the high point of which was the Russian tea Mollie served us with so much affection and attention, and always a sliver of lemon, like a kind of ritual, in their tiny kitchen. It was the only place during the whole of our time in Mexico where I ever came across tea. I vividly recall the whole performance, carried out as though this was the one small but important rite, which still connected them to their native Russia.

At this time I was five, six and seven. At our new home in Mexico – a small flat on the fifth floor of an orange-yellow apartment building – my mother was out working, often days and nights. I remember standing on a chair by the gas stove and frying an egg for myself, the way she had taught me and content with my accomplishment, when I got home to the small empty flat every day after school. I would sit down to my snack and find ways to pass the time and amuse myself until my mother came in, wan and tired, when it was already getting dark.

Our visits to Senya and Mollie were a highlight, and a connection to our Serpa Pinto days. There are photos in my album of me sitting on Mollie's lap, on the deck of the ship, and one of my mother, tall and slim, bordering on undernourished from our years in France, Mollie, tiny and ebullient, and I, the smallest, at five years old. We are posing for the camera on the ship's deck, the three of us standing close together against the

Mollie Steimer, Käte, and Miriam on the Serpa Pinto, 1941

railing with the sea behind us.

Senya had soon established a photographic studio on the seventh floor – I seem to remember – of a building, close to a busy intersection overlooked by the statue of Cuauhtémoc, near the centre of Mexico City.

Senya's photographs hung all along the length of the brightly lit corridor that ran from their minimal living quarters to the spacious photographic studio at the back of the apartment. His photographs were also in permanent exhibition in Mexico City's main concert hall and cultural centre, El Palacio

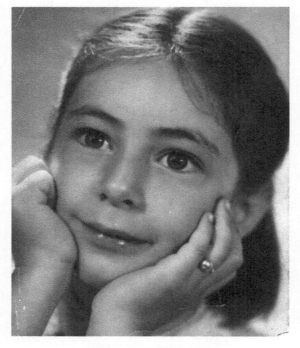

Miriam, photo SEMO, 1942

de Bellas Artes. Studies in black and white of the Ballet Russe de Monte Carlo, catching the movement of the dancers, singly or in groups, portraits of Alicia Markova and Anton Dolin, of the opera singer Maria Callas, and of other international and Mexican stars of the theatre and cinema, as well as images capturing the indigenous beauty and character of women and children and other subjects in their Mexican ambience.

Senya Flechine and Mollie Steimer were Russian anarchists. Many of their idealistic group of friends and acquaintances that had come to Mexico were anarchist or some variant of anti-Stalinist Marxism. Some twenty years earlier, around the time of the First World War, Mollie had been imprisoned in the

United States with several of her friends, including one named Jacob Abrams, for distributing leaflets that were considered unpatriotic. They were requesting an end to American military intervention and assistance to Tsarist Russia, from which they had just fled, against what they then saw as – and would later revise – the people's revolution. Their early release from their fifteen and twenty year sentences was obtained by the justices Oliver Wendell Holmes and Louis Brandeis who cited the American constitution and their right to free speech in what

Mary and Jack Abrams, Rose Pesotta, Senya Flechine and Mollie Steimer

became known as the case, *Abrams v. United States.*

I remember Jacob Abrams in Mexico. I can still see him, a convivial, spirited figure with flopping hair and a beaming smile, spilling over with warmth and attention towards everyone around him. He always engaged with me playfully and affectionately when we visited him and his wife Mary.

Following their discharge from prison and deportation from the United States, in the early 1920s, Mollie returned to Russia to join in the revolution but was again imprisoned, along with Senya this time, for their anti-Bolshevik sentiments and activities. From victims of the Red Scare in America, they became victims of the Red Terror in Russia, as has been so aptly recorded. The conditions of their Russian jails, including time in solitary confinement, were barbaric and led to Mollie's hunger strikes. They were eventually released, this time with the help of Maxim Gorky's girlfriend, and deported once again, on this occasion from their original homeland, Russia. From there they went on to become part of the cultural life in Berlin and, when the Nazis took over, in Paris.

A leading woman anarchist thinker of the time described Mollie as, "diminutive and quaint... with an iron will and a tender heart", and of her prosecution in America, she wrote, "the entire machinery of the United States government was being employed to crush this slip of a girl weighing less than eighty pounds."

We also visited Gustav Regler and his wife Marie Louise in their beautiful Spanish colonial home in the city's district of San Angel. I remember friendly, pleasant afternoons when coffee was served for the adults and long discussions took place around a table under the shade of a large tree in their garden. Regler had also been in Spain during the Spanish Civil War where he had fought in the International Brigade and led some crucial battles in the front against Franco's armies.

Gustav Regler with Hemingway and Ilya Ehrenburg, in Spain during the Civil War

Marie Louise came from Worpswede, the northwestern German town where – as chance would have it – the young Kortokraks would meet her family, the Vogelers, as well as Gustav Regler, whose portrait he painted during his years there after the war in Europe.

Like Jacob Abrams, Regler too was always thoughtfully attentive and affectionately playful with me. I enjoyed and looked forward to our visits to Gustav and Marie Louise. Until one memorable, very hot, sunny afternoon. He was tinkering around, on this occasion, stripped to the waist, fixing his flowerbed in the garden, while Marie Louise was setting our places on the table under the shady tree. He had been teasing and splashing me with the water hose he was using on the flowerbed, and I – responding to his playful antics – waited for him to turn around from the flowerbed, and pointed the hose at him, squirting him in his bare chest... There was a moment's ominous silence, followed by complete panic. He went berserk, and twitched and screamed at me like a wild animal gone mad. I stood there, unable to move, suddenly feeling very, very frightened. Every sinew of my small body felt stretched and taut and confused and bewildered. Never before or since have I experienced anything anywhere close to such an intense, primal, gut fear. The rest of the afternoon remained tense, bleak and sombre for the whole company, with none of the happy, animated exchanges and chatter of other times.

I had to wait a few years before my mother decided I was grown up enough for her to explain to me Regler's response that afternoon. It turned out that when the cold water hit his chest, Regler thought my mother had shot him. He appears to have been in a continuous state of fear for his life, ever since he had defected from the Communist Party following Stalin's pact with Hitler. My mother had also left the Party, some time earlier, while still in Spain. Having personally witnessed the fates of dissidents and defectors, and being acquainted with the driven mindset and forces that dealt with them and the methods in place, it would seem that Regler couldn't truly trust anyone anymore.

Around this time, my mother started working at the Café Vienna in Mexico City's Colonia Roma where many of the refugees from Europe had settled. My mother planned and prepared the evening meals and served the large clientele of refugees single-handedly, while I roamed and amused myself in the big park, Parque Mexico, across the road from the café and our new living quarters above it. I remember the large numbers of people, many of them friends and acquaintances from our

Serpa Pinto days, that congregated and socialised at the café around a European meal in the Austro-German tradition, giving them a collective sense of home. The home they had left behind in Europe and were nostalgically trying to resurrect, or at best bring back some semblance of the ambience of their past life, recover some flavours and nuances of it on this side of the Atlantic. The café was their meeting point, where they could indulge in the dishes of their past, reminisce and socialise together in their new country. In my incorrigible curiosity, I would strain to see and grasp the sentiment of the assembled group, many of them familiar faces and habitual customers, from a distance in the park, since my mother had made the café strictly out of bounds for me, so as not to interfere with her demanding work and its smooth running.

In the afternoons, when I came home from school, she would already be preparing for the influx of diners she would be attending to later that evening. I would cross the road to Parque México and while away the time getting to know its every nook and cranny. I enjoyed roaming all over it on a rented, park bicycle, and play with the other local children until they were called in for their supper; I would then immerse myself in my make-believe world in certain favourite spots, or try out the swings and slides in the children's playground at the other end of the park. It would be late and getting dark already by the time my mother called me in, ready to give me my supper, and sit me down to do my homework for the next day.

One woman of my mother's age often stayed behind to chat and spend time with her. She was tall and slim, had blue eyes and straight lanky hair, and always wore suits and gloves. I became used to seeing her in my mother's company: Ilse became a good friend and confidante. Or so it seemed. The future would tell a different story.

As well as the Café Vienna, my mother took on additional jobs. At first she would do night shift work at a nearby hospital or clinic. Later, I remember waiting for her sometimes at the bus stop further up alongside Parque Mexico, across the street. She never told me where she went or what she worked at, or anything about the people she met or of her experiences away from home. Maybe she was simply too exhausted to communicate any of this when she finally reached our small flat at the end of her long day, or she thought it would be of no interest to me, or that I was too young for her to share it with me. I recently discovered that some of her absences at the time were to give French and English lessons at a Mexican evening business school. I found this bit of information in some papers she left behind, with an account of her wide and varied activities in search of a livelihood during her lifetime. She appears to have drawn up this list in her later years, in her attempt to get a pension from the authorities in Germany, taking into account the interruption of her profession by her enforced life of exile as a result of that country's then racial policies and all that followed.

With her training in paediatric nursing, she had obtained positions tending the children of distinguished personalities in Berlin, London, Barcelona and New York. She had looked after the child of the Berlin lawyer and writer, Heinrich Alexander-Katz; the British geneticist Lionel Penrose's son Oliver; the Catalan historian Agustí Duran i San Pere's daughter Lali; and in Mexico she was engaged to mind Léonide Massine's infant daughter, Tatiana, when he was presenting his new ballet, Aleko, with the Ballet Russe de Monte Carlo and

Chagall's sets and costumes at the Palacio de Bellas Artes, in the autumn of 1942.

It was maybe over the weekends, when I was not at school, that my mother took me along with her. I remember how she would disappear into the palatial villa where she looked after Massine's daughter, after leaving me at the entrance of the large marquee, in the huge flower filled gardens, with strict instructions to make myself unheard and invisible. I would stand glued to the wall just inside the entrance watching Massine take the dancers through their steps at rehearsal, utterly still and spell bound. Dancing had become my greatest

Leonide Massine rehearsing Aleko in Mexio, 1942

passion, and I longed one day to become a dancer like those beautiful, ethereal, perfect creatures, who moved so gracefully in unison with the music, in their creations of sheer magic.

Back at the Café Vienna, my mother's European cooking and menus were greatly appreciated. Her German *apfelkuchen* and cheesecake were legendary, and remained so, long after our days in Mexico. I have never tasted any that surpassed them. She made a delicious shortcrust pastry, and added sultanas, ground nuts, sugar and cinnamon to the coarsely grated apple. She would top the whole thing with fine strips from the left-over pastry laid over the apple in an open basket weave pattern, adding a final layer of sugar, cinnamon and flaked almonds. For the cheese cake she used quark or curd cheese blended with sugar, cream and egg yolks, into which she folded beaten egg whites and added lemon zest. Not even the New York cheesecakes I have tasted match up to it.

The Café Vienna became a regular meeting ground for the European refugees concentrated in Colonia Roma, many of whom had come on the Serpo Pinto and formed a close-knit artistic and politically active refugee community. Among them were the three women surrealist artists Leonora Carrington, Kati Horna and Remedios Varo, along with their lovers and husbands-to-be Chiki Weisz and Benjamin Péret, who had also been on the same voyage of the Serpa Pinto with my mother and me. I met Kati again on my subsequent visits to Mexico at her home, still in Colonia Roma, her warmth and liveliness ever spilling over. Her stark, earthy photography of people's suffering in the Spanish Civil War turned in Mexico into compelling photographic images of surrealistic thought and fantasy in close collaboration with her inseparable friend and surrealist painter Leonora Carrington. Carrington had eloped with Max Ernst from her respectable English home, spent a heady, creative time in Paris with the surrealists, followed by a harrowing breakdown in Spain, before she sought refuge in Mexico.

In the turbulent world and age they were living in, their discussions and writing, along with their explorations and experimentations in their art, were all part of their search for new meanings and interpretations and a better world. They formed a close association with the other painters and muralists in Mexico, Diego Rivera, Frida Kahlo, Siqueiros and Orozco. The relationship between radical art and revolutionary politics was integral to these Mexican painters, following the impact of the Mexican Revolution, coincident with the Russian Revolution, barely two or three decades previously: they conceived their works as an art for the people. These artists and intellectuals would also fall out with each other when their ideologies diverged, sometimes leading to insurmountable disagreements and break-ups. As, for instance, when Siqueiros was implicated in the attempt on Trotsky's life, the wall above his bed profusely pitted from the shots to this day.

Other members of their group, back to their pre-war years in Paris, and an integral part of André Breton's inner circle, were Wolfgang Paalen and his wife Alice Rahon. They had been invited to Mexico by Frida Kahlo, whom they had befriended in Paris, during her visit there a few years earlier. Diego Rivera and Frida Kahlo installed them in a house next to Frida's *Casa Azul* – now a museum and open to the public – in Mexico City's district of Coyoacan.

In the summer of 1943, Wolfgang Paalen became very ill and my mother was engaged to attend to him. In the same way

Wolfgang Paalen in his studio in Mexico

as, in the previous year, she took me along when she was looking after Léonide Massine's baby daughter, and left me to watch him take his dancers through their rehearsal, I recall my mother taking me to Paalen's home and leaving me in the care of Alice, while she attended to Paalen's nursing needs. Alice was very beautiful, she had a lovely, natural, open look and smile, and wore her chestnut coloured hair softly wrapped around her head.

I remember her as gentle and attentive when she sat with me in the large tropical garden, full of exotic trees and flowers and cacti, with pre-Columbian and Amerindian sculptures placed in various chosen positions to give them prominence and at the same time allow them to blend naturally into their surroundings. The object that seemed to captivate Alice most, though, and she drew my attention to every time, was her marten. The brown furry animal was attached by a very long rope to the trunk of a tree, and ran around as much of the

Alice Rahon

garden as the rope allowed.

Nicole's neighbour in Paris, Georgiana Colvile, has written about Alice Rahon and her art. In her book, *Scandaleusement d'elles*, on thirty-four Dadaist and surrealist women painters, there is a candid sunny photograph of Alice, taken by Roland Penrose, and a sample of her art work, which I see as a rich display full of whimsical, poetic charm with undertones of Klee and Miró.

Wolfgang Paalen started an art magazine, *DYN*, which was distributed in New York, Paris and London, and gathered an elite artistic international following. As well as art works, it published philosophical essays, photography, poems and archeological and anthropological articles relating to Mexico and Canadian Amerindian cultures: the mystery, legend and magic of their surviving artefacts lending themselves to the Surrealists' focus on the world of symbols, dreams and imagination. Paalen broke away from his Surrealist beginnings at this time, and his paintings, which featured in the *DYN* magazine, became studies of rhythm, light and colour in the genre of Abstract Expressionism. Breton broke his relations with him as a consequence, and Paalen now established himself with Peggy Guggenheim and her circle. My mother obtained all the issues of the *DYN* magazine, produced from 1941 to 1944, and took them with her in her subsequent travels.

I must have been seven years old around the time my mother was nursing Paalen. In the same year, we made new friends in our circle of Spanish refugees. It was probably Mollie and Senya, who would have known them through their network of anarchist friends and acquaintances and who had introduced them to my mother, perhaps with the idea of presenting me to a playmate with some common background outside school.

Vicenta and El Nano were an earthy working couple at the core of the anti-Franco sentiment in Spain. I remember Vicenta as a kind, strong, down-to-earth and utterly practical woman. She was squat and sturdy with short, permed, greying hair and a fixing, no-nonsense look in her clear, direct eyes. Her life companion, El Nano, was tall and steely, rather handsome, with a head of tight, black curls and eyes of a deep brown tinged with blue-grey which radiated a blend of strength and kindness. Their daughter, Liber – short for Libertad, or Liberty, a commonly given name to children of the Spanish Civil War, and the sentiment for which they were fighting – was my age by two weeks. Liber was not Vicenta and El Nano's biological child. Her real mother had died when Liber was a baby and her father was tortured and killed by Franco's men. Since then, Vicenta and El Nano had taken care of Liber as though she were their own child and had brought her with them to Mexico when they fled Spain.

They lived in Texcoco, a town on the other side of the great lake Mexico City is built on. The same lake that, according to legend, the wandering Aztecs, in search of a new place to settle, had found with the omen of an eagle, perched on a cactus, devouring a snake, on an island in the middle of the lake. That marked the spot where they were to build their new city, Tenochtitlán, which reached its pinnacle when the Spanish Conquistadors discovered it, two hundred years later, and described it as unequalled in wonder to anything they knew or had previously seen. Before they proceeded to destroy it and build their own capital on its ruins.

In the days I spent at Vicenta and El Nano's with Liber, Texcoco was an old Spanish colonial town with unpaved roads bordered by austere, high, stone walls which hid palatial homes and gardens. Liber and her parents, in contrast, lived in a simple brick construction of two rooms: a bedroom and a living-work room. The cooking was done outside in the yard, and the primitive lavatory was further back. The yard was full of domestic and farm animals: dogs, cats, chickens, turkeys, pigs, and two goats. I would go and stay with them in Texcoco during my school holidays, which would give me the company of my new friend, and my mother the greater freedom to follow her work's demands.

I enjoyed playing with Liber. She became my best friend. I also took in and readily adapted to my new rustic surroundings, our closeness to the earth and the primal sources of our day-to-day needs and living. I would watch Vicenta make chorizo. After laboriously mincing the meat of one of their animals by hand and mixing it with various condiments, Vicenta would squeeze the spicy mixture with its pungent, peppery smell into interminably long strips of animal gut, which she had cleaned and prepared beforehand. Finally, she would hang the long stuffed tubes of gut in loops to dry in the yard. Vicenta would put aside a whole day for this job.

After two to three years in this, our new country, my life was falling into a rhythm. My mother, on the other hand, must have still been struggling to provide for both of us and rebuild her life. My father suddenly reappears on the scene now, and changes everything.

We were delighted to have him back. I, for one, was jubilant. Though my meetings with him had been so few and far between, I had always felt a great affection for him and kept some especially fond memories of him. And my mother was, I believe, glad and relieved to finally have some emotional support as well as his practical assistance after her years of hardship. In spite of the many enduring friendships she made in every new place and circumstance, I believe — now looking back — she must have had many moments of great loneliness.

A recently discovered letter in her belongings, which she left behind after her death, throws new light on what must have been her state of mind when my father appeared again in Mexico and joined us.

The letter is from Alexander Granach. It is hand-written, two pages long, headed from "254 South Amalfi Drive, Santa Monica, California". Amalfi Drive is a lengthy road that cuts through Hollywood's legendary Sunset Boulevard, and the address he gives is close to Santa Monica beach along the Pacific coast. He writes it is five in the morning, he has just got up, and the first thing he is doing is addressing her. He wants her to know how much he honoured her and how much she meant to him from the moment they first met and got to know each other, recalling their swims together "in the stormy sea". Could this have been the same stormy seas in her photograph album of Helgoland, which my mother used to visit when she was in her teens, and where Granach was acting in *Nosferatu*? He reflects on the passage of time since those days, and on the need to hang on and be strong in the face of the terrible fates and suffering by so many, from all that had befallen in those intervening years. He writes about his work in Hollywood, his writing and impending publication in English of his autobiographical novel, *Da geht ein Mensch*, translated into *There Goes an Actor*, and of his latest prominent role in the film *Hangmen Also Die*, which he highly commends and urges her to see if it comes to Mexico. And he adds, translated from German:

> *...And now tell me in detail about yourself... what you have done in the last ten years, and how you came to end up in Mexico. And whether you can come to me in America. And what can I do for you. And how big is your daughter and allow me to love her from my heart even before I have seen her, write to me simply everything about yourself. And how you see your-self there, and how you live... It is such a peaceful morning... write to me a long and full account of yourself, because every-thing interests me – because you are very dear to me my brave Katinka – and thank you for your signs of life – the world is not so thickly sown with friendships, but those there are, those who feel it, should hang together.*
>
> *As I will, and as you should, with your old, Alexei.*

Though it is not dated, from his references to the films in which he acted, and those that had just come out, as well as his not yet published book, the letter must have been written around the time when my father joined us again in Mexico. If so, the timing couldn't have been more ill-matched and com-plicated... I cannot imagine what she must have felt and gone through on receiving it.

The last time we had seen my father had been in Marseilles, at the end of 1941, before we embarked on the Serpa Pinto. My father had stayed behind in France. Even though he was Jewish, his American citizenship had protected him from the

Vichy French and the occupying Germans, until the Americans entered the war. At the time of my mother's departure from France with me, he was overseeing homes administered by the Quakers for the care of Spanish children refugees. I have recently discovered, in a document entitled *The American Friends Service Records Relating to Humanitarian Work in France*, that, as the war progressed and more children were endangered, he was placed in charge of emigration. Archived carbon copies of his letters – written in equally fluent and flawless French, English, or Spanish, though none of these were his mother tongue – show that he had studied the problems presented by each individual request and then advised, negotiated, coordinated and procured the necessary papers and expenses for the transport of many desperate adults and children to the United States and Mexico. As well as a large group of children, from Spanish refugees, he had sent to America for adoption, he also assisted with the flight of many orphaned Jewish children, whose parents had been sent to their deaths in the concentration camps, as part of the One Thousand Children rescue programme.

His magnanimous and dedicated assistance to so many was, however, marred by two notable exceptions: his wife and daughter. In papers I found after her death, my mother referred to receiving our lifesaving financial help and documents for our transit to Mexico from a Swiss Jewish aid organisation. Among other intractable problems in their relationship and mismatch of character, something of a tug-of-war over me, when we were in France, may have soured their relations to the extent that he became blinded to the danger we faced. Or the explanation lies more simply in their relations having hit rock bottom and their misunderstandings reached an insurmountable chasm.

My mother and I were crossing the Atlantic on the Serpa Pinto, when the Japanese attacked Pearl Harbour, on the morning of the 7th of December, 1941, and the United States declared war against Japan and Germany. It would take about a year before the Germans, fearing the American advance, overran and took control of the free zone in Vichy France, and my father was no longer safe. He was eventually caught and interned by the Germans in Baden-Baden, in the Brenner Park Hotel – a vast and elegant residence with a spa, surrounded by well-tended gardens and an extensive park, at other, more normal times patronised by royalty, the rich and the famous – along with members from the American Friends he had been working with, and some American Embassy officials and other notables. But not before he had made an extraordinary – bordering on the quixotic – attempt to cross into the neutral territory of Switzerland, which his roommate at the Brenner Park internment hotel, Burritt Hiatt, wrote in his published diary.

Hiatt reports on Louis Frank's account of how, on realising he was on the brink of capture by the Germans, he had taken a train from Marseilles to Chamonix and set off alone and on foot, in the pouring rain, blindly following mountain trails and sheep tracks right through the pitch-dark, moonless night to avoid detection, intent on reaching the Swiss border. He knew it was mountainous terrain, but had not counted on the steep peaks, precipitous cliffs, and other obstacles he was faced with in the darkness. By morning he found a rocky ledge to sleep under – intending to continue his march when it became dark again, to avoid the guards – to be soon woken by a dog sniffing his face, in bright daylight. It belonged to a French border guard who marched him to the patrol headquarters and put him on a donkey back to Chamonix, from where he arrived back in Marseilles two weeks after he thought he had departed from it.

At the Brenner Park Hotel, Jews were not accommodated among the internees, and in all likelihood he would have been sent to Gurs – one of the concentration camps in France, in transit to the extermination camps in Poland – had his friends not rallied around, vouched for him, and managed to prevent it.

Of the adults my father had assisted, he mentioned having helped the lapsed Bolshevik writer Victor Serge to emigrate to Mexico. It would be some thirty or more years later that my father would buy a section of land in Cuernavaca with his son, the artist Vlady Serge, where they each built a house of their own in their part of the land, and lived as friends and neighbours.

Our family life together, when my father joined us in Mexico towards the end of the war, was short lived. Without any warning or preparation that I remember, though I expect my mother and father must have discussed it between them, he took my mother and me and left us in an outlying village of dirt roads, mud huts and weekend villas, on the edge of Cuernavaca: about two hours' drive from Mexico City, at the time. My father stayed in the city and would occasionally visit us on the weekends.

That was the end of my treasured schooling, adored ballet and flamenco classes, cherished friends, and the way of life I had become accustomed to and was by now appreciating and enjoying in Mexico city. And, over time, the start of my new love affair with Acapantzingo's untamed Mexican countryside and indigenous life in all its wild exuberance, as I explored and absorbed it in the intensity of my dawning adolescence. I came to delight in the brilliant clashing colours; the irresistible lively music and the ballads and songs that told of life, love, death, and the inimitable patriotic devotion to Mexico; the strongly scented dazzling flowers, tangled tropical leafy greenery and jungle of the towering ancient trees; every kind of animal, domestic and wild – the more dangerous of which, the ubiquitous scorpions and snakes, I learnt how to evade and guard against.

Soon after our arrival in Acapantzingo, I found out that my mother was pregnant, expecting my father's second child following their short rapprochement in Mexico City. I had turned nine years old when my sister Evelyn was born. My mother went to Mexico City for the birth and my father was by her side throughout her long and difficult labour. He would continue to spend weekends in Acapantzingo with us, but they were never to get together again.

My mother's friend from her Café Vienna days, Ilse, was having an affair with my father. I saw little of him anymore, and when I did there wasn't the connection or the warm, close exchanges we had once had, of which I still had a nebulous, deep memory, on the occasions when he had visited us in Spain and France. And as I approached my adolescence and stood at the threshold of my own, more adult world, my mother too was becoming more alienated from me. Difficulties in our relationship had already begun to appear in Mexico City, before my father's arrival, when I was seven years old, and I was starting to assert my autonomy. Our increasingly different preoccupations in life now were driving a deeper wedge between us, and our communication – once so close – was breaking up.

In this, my most recent change and new surroundings, I would wander through our own vicinity and beyond, becoming familiar with every dirt street, view and corner in Acapantzingo, the collections of mud huts where the indigenous people lived and the weekend villas of wealthy Mexicans from the city, the wild unkempt abandoned sections of land and the lush cultivated tropical gardens, the local school down the road, the small chapel further on, and the cemetery where they buried their children and celebrated the day of the dead, with the distant volcanoes Popocatepetl and Ixtacihuatl shimmering in the bright sunshine.

I would walk into Cuernavaca, and go into the Palacio de Cortés to look at the Diego Rivera's murals that covered the length of the walls in the large terrace overlooking the part of town on the other side of the barranca and the volcanoes beyond. I would look at every detail in the paintings depicting the history of Mexico, from the life and heroes of its pre-Columbian past, on to their defeat by the Spanish Conquistadors, up to the present mestizo life and society. Humble, illiterate, indigenous men would be standing there too, in their white cotton clothing, hat in hand and barefoot, looking long and hard at the paintings depicting their history.

For also here in Mexico there had been a revolution in the early twentieth century, which had removed the autocratic ruler Porfirio Diaz and aimed to give more power to the people – though the change seemed to have slowed down, even arrested, as the totalitarian leader was replaced by the corrupt, one-party government of the *Partido Revolucionario Institucional*, which ruled for the greater part of the twentieth century. And here was a mural illustrating the entire chronicle of events, exemplifying art's engagement with the social and political questions here in Mexico.

In a recent visit to Mexico, I returned to Cuernavaca and the Palacio de Cortés, in my attempt to recover something of that intense life experience of my childhood. I found the palace had been turned into a museum which exhibits the history of the area, from the mammoth bones discovered in the region, across the various native tribes who populated and fought here, through the Spanish conquest and colonisers, right up to a room exhibiting early photographs of Cuernavaca, some of them with the renowned revolutionary, Emiliano Zapata. And, in these black and white photographs I was standing in front of, I recognised a Cuernavaca much closer to the one stored in my memories than the one I see around me today. I realised then, that my life there, and the Cuernavaca I experienced and knew, have become part of history.

In those days, in front of our home in Acapantzingo, a path led to a cattle ranch behind the collection of mud huts across the street from our house. We became friends with Conchita, who ran the ranch at the end of the path, where the ground started sloping into the barranca. She had frequent visitors from Mexico City who came to stay. One of these was a pretty young woman called Kitty, with a mane of curly brown hair and a lovely smile. Kitty was the great grand-daughter of Porfirio Diaz. No longer privileged now, Kitty's main preoccupation was her nose, which she was forever hiding behind her hand, though I couldn't have faulted it.

My mother's friendships were deep and loyal, and spread across different backgrounds, classes, cultures, nationalities and ideologies. It was ultimately the individual person that mattered. And as great a rapport as she built up with such a broad selection of friends, her talent for understanding and tolerance broke down when it came to me, her daughter: we misconnected and misinterpreted each other until we lost sight of our meeting point. Maybe our histories had been too close and joined up, for her to be able to see me dispassionately.

As for me, I had experienced a huge measure of life, colour, music, history, art and humanity, during my six formative years in Mexico, all of which became an essential part of me. If one looks carefully at Kortokraks's unfinished portrait, beyond the pain and confusion in the eye, one can maybe discover a bit of Mexico there.

An Unfinished Portrait

The jet of water crashes down on me, bracing and energising, as I prepare myself for a new day. Here under the shower, with water spurting and sloshing every which way, words spring forth unprompted and form themselves into fluent phrases and formulations that express what I was trying to compose, less successfully, at the end of the day, last night.

On the facing wall of the blue bathroom hangs the framed poster of Degas' drawing of a woman after her bath. She is leaning forward on her cane chair, drying the back of her neck with a large soft towel and revealing, as she does so, her beautiful slim-waisted back down to the firm, soft curve of her hips. The picture's colours of flesh and blues pleasingly match the blue glass tiles that line the length and breadth of the bathroom.

Wrapped in my thick towel, fresh out of the shower and still wet, I now sit on the sofa recording the groups of words that formed and flitted through my head while I washed. Lest I lose them if I delay to note them down. Water flowing and streaming over my soapy body setting the mind free, mental blocks dissolving and ideas soaring and jostling for expression as I stood encircled by misting mirrors and the large cerulean glass tiles, their blueness invoking the sea and the sky into the room. I grabbed the towel and came to my place by the window, where I face the light spacious room inside and the whirling luminous clouds drifting over the glinting river below, on the other side of the plate glass. A flock of gulls is taking off from the riverbank, wings fluttering, gliding and soaring into the air, in a display of exaltation and freedom. My computer on my lap, I try to note everything down before the formulated ideas slither away and disappear like a freshly caught fish slipping through one's hands back into the water.

Transforming memories, scenes, ideas and impressions into a verbal account requires going into the very essence of their meaning or sensation, to find the words that most closely and evocatively express and convey them, rather as I imagine a painter becomes immersed right inside the nature of the image and character of what will be transposed, with oils, pastels or mixed media, onto paper or canvas.

In Serifos, I have trekked with Panos to the top of the mountain overlooking the natural harbour of Koutalas below, once used for the exportation of iron from the island's mines, and now a small fishing village. On the summit, we come across an abundance of shards from a previous, ancient world, lying around everywhere we look. There are earthenware pieces and handles that at one time formed jugs and plates, and other artefacts: I try to imagine what they might have once looked like and, beyond them, what this now bare hill top covered with scrub and some scattered shrubs and bushes might have appeared like in a bygone era, when it was a bustling town or city.

In the same way an archaeologist attempts to reconstruct the past from the few fragments he or she is able to dig up, recover and patch together, I have tried to piece together my mother's life. Though many components may not fit and will challenge understanding, and many details will be lost or missing, and the picture remain incomplete.

This story is about lives and history that remain unresolved and, here and there, present contradictions. I have focused on my mother in my attempt to compose a portrait of her from my memories, her photographs, my return to her homes and haunts, and an exploration of the complicated and changing worlds she experienced and inhabited. A portrait that will for ever remain unfinished, though I hope I have captured some gist of a woman caught in the middle of critical events of the twentieth century and their profound effect on her and her whole existence, events that have now receded with her into history. I wished to explore how chance, history and the individual meet and interact, making them what they become. Even so, what I describe here is, of course, not my mother, but my vision of her, the way I imagine her from my sifting reflections and careful perusal of the photo albums she created, with so much care and dedication, from her collection of photographs that record her experiences from the time she left her parental home and started an independent life of her own. They are a testimony of her hospital training, work and companions, her travels and adventures, her friends, her loves, her passions, and all the meaningful activities of her young life up till the time she was caught up and snagged in two wars and left with nothing other than her small daughter, me, some essential possessions, and her photo albums which she took with her wherever she went, intent on preserving our lives, her photographs and her memories. All she had left that confirmed she had had a past.

My father didn't have a past. Or rather, he had erased it. From his consciousness and his memory. He remembered he had once been a small boy who would climb trees and steal apples to complement the lunch he bought with the kopek his mother gave him every morning, when setting off from the small farmstead his widowed mother ran, and where she looked after her eight children, to his school in the village. But when I asked what his name had once been, he would say he didn't know. Or what was the family surname, he couldn't remember. He was nine years old when his older brothers, who had already emigrated to America to escape from their declining agrarian life, difficult times, and random pogroms in Lithuania, sent for him and his mother and remaining sister. At nine, you know and remember your name.

My father didn't have photograph albums. He didn't have photographs. Apart from a single one he once, in a rare moment, showed me of himself as a small boy with curly earlocks and a kippah on his head. And then, all the family's documents were lost when the Bible in which they were kept fell into a river from the boat they were travelling in, on their way to a German port, before sailing to New York. And so it was that they left all record of their identities behind and acquired a new family name, and new first names, and new birth dates as they best remembered, when they disembarked in Ellis Island at the start of the twentieth century. As my father grew older and took note of his new surroundings in New York, he decided on his Bar Mitzvah – which gave him the authority to determine his future course – to give up and distance himself from his Jewish religion and customs.

According to a Mexican film director's research for a docudrama she made based on his life, who travelled all the way from Mexico to the small Lithuanian village of Prienai to search through its archives, my father's name was probably Ruven-Leiba Frock before he became Louis Frank. And my paternal grandparents, whom I never knew nor did they ever know me, were Itzek and Gitta. I note it here so that this earlier part of their lives and identities may not be forgotten after all. Itzek and Gitta.

My father was what one would describe as a self-made man. He was an eager, diligent and outstanding pupil as he went through the vast, crowded, all boys' high school in the immigrant, working-class, West Side district of Manhattan. He went on to attend Cornell University to read Humanities, with a special interest in Philosophy, but his studies were interrupted by his draft in the First World War, where his initiative and exceptional grasp of languages led to his recruitment into counterintelligence. My mother in contrast had a solid European background rooted in its rich, well established culture and traditions. All that – along with their profoundly different natures: my father's easy and laid back, compared with my mother's more fervent and exacting behaviour and expectations – may, I believe, underlie their gross incompatibility.

Though my father mentions, in notes he left behind, that he had determined as a young boy to lead a pure and virtuous life and remain abstinent till marriage, as he grew older his intentions appear to have broken down and instead he embarked on many affairs. I met my French sister, Edith, for the first time recently. Her mother had been in charge of one of the Quakers' children's camps that my father was overseeing – La Rouvière, near Marseilles – during the Second World War, and she was born the year after my mother and I left France for Mexico. Another sister, Evelyn, born when my father rejoined us, briefly, in Mexico, is my only full sibling, though she is much younger than me, born at a time when I was already breaking away into my own separate life and activities, leading to different occupations and histories. My father had two more children with Ilse, after we left for New Zealand, my Mexican siblings, José and Susana. To complete the picture, during his early years in Spain and before he met my mother in Barcelona, he had a little girl and twins from a liaison with a young Valencian woman, but all three sadly died in infancy.

As he moved on from Reuven-Leiba Frock to Louis Frank, my father's views and outlook must have undergone considerable transformation. As much or as little as I saw of him, and observed and struggled to understand him, he appears before me like the wonderfully heroic, part ingenious, part ingenuous, Don Quixote, in some ways also a Walter Mitty, and in others a Schindler, all three rolled into one. He did, in fact, greatly admire Miguel de Cervantes's *Don Quijote de la Mancha* as a literary flight of adventures that most resonated with him.

I have here in my hand a beautiful, gold embossed, leather-bound, boutique, Spanish edition of *Don Quijote de la Mancha*, with very fine paper and elegant print, which my father dedicated to me on our departure from Mexico in 1948, on our way to New Zealand. That was when my parents' relations were once again at their lowest ebb.

Not only was I shocked to learn, bit by bit, as I grew older, what had awaited us had we not managed to escape from France, and what actually did happen to the others who hadn't made it, but on top of the threats and dangers from the war, other dramas were being played out, more personal in nature and, to a child, also highly disturbing. We were not only subjected to the fear of political and racial persecutions and roundups, and the looming threat of the extermination camps, but were also faced with all the heartache and deprivation that arose from the monumental misunderstandings within a family. When my parents' relations broke down again, and for a last time, after their brief reunion in Mexico at the end of the war, I was of an age – at ten and eleven

– in which these dramas and personal antagonisms between those closest to me had an especially unsettling effect, and my mother's pain and once more disillusionment and bitterness against my father, had rubbed off on me. I had seen little of my father during my life up till then, while she had been my constant presence, and I naturally felt her distress and took her side.

So I didn't pick up and take in my father's dedication inside the pages of this precious miniature edition of *Don Quijote* he was presenting me with, on this, our renewed departure.

Miriam,
Este buen compañero de viaje te doy
sabiendo que te divertirá mucho,
te instruyerá bastante, y espero,
te iluminará un poco en el sendero
de la eterna ilusión de bondad,
ternura y amor.
Tu papa
Mexico, 18 enero 1948

Miriam
This good travel companion, I give you with
the knowledge that it will amuse you greatly,
instruct you considerably, and, I hope,
illuminate you a little along the eternal
visionary path to kindness,
tenderness and love.
Your daddy
Mexico, 18 January, 1948

Rereading it now, both of them, my father and mother, now dead, my realisation of the warmth, good will and caring that are manifested in his words have shaken me. What is more, I notice that the facing page has been torn out, suggesting this small volume had been his own, cherished edition, maybe given and dedicated to him by someone he held dear, which he, in turn, had been carrying around with him in his own travels, all of which made his choice to part from it and give it to me all the more precious. This observation, along with these same words, so thoughtfully written for me, which I would have read at the time, must have slipped clean past my notice and attention in my state of temporary blindness, brought on by my feeling of having been let down, along with my mother, and abandoned. An emotional blindness precipitated by the personal drama around me, which had absorbed and enveloped me with its sense of lost love and heightened disillusion, and a need to start again. Departures and new starts had become part of our lives and I tended to take them in my stride, but this last one seemed to hit harder, maybe as I was growing older I was also becoming more aware of the nature of the events that drove them. Though I had not yet grasped their many sided complexities.

It would not be long before the remaining fragile connection I had with my mother would also break down completely. I am looking here at two photographs taken many years later. I am married, have two small children of my own, and we are attending the private view of an exhibition of Kortokraks works. I am wearing a modish, black, embroidered mini dress and am exotically made up with a rim of Kohl around my eyes and the then fashionable beehive hairstyle. I am looking straight ahead in the direction of the camera, oblivious of my mother next to me who is gazing at me with a strange, puzzled, questioning, almost anguished, look, as though trying to fathom me, a mix of admiration, incomprehension, sadness and what... Love maybe? Which she was struggling with and didn't know how to express? Followed by the next photograph in the same position, where she has managed a smile.

The frozen image caught and suspended by the camera can be studied at will. The body's pose, the tilt of the head, the facial expression, the eyes' look at that split second, may, on occasions, reveal what up till then was an unknown stance, or unsuspected emotions.

Maybe I represented to her the family and home she had lost, and she could not understand our estrangement. While to me, she was the mother I had once felt intimately connected with and then discarded by, unable to accept me for who I was. Her need to mould me in her image when my mould was another, and her mistaking independence of spirit for an absence of love... A common misconception perhaps, but much intensified in our situation by our history of frequent uprooting, losses and unsettled lives.

So much misunderstanding. Missed meeting points, forever at cross purposes, facing divergent directions, never listening for the unsaid. My mother's so fundamentally mistaken belief that I would not be interested in her photographs. These albums I have been poring over and describing here in my attempt to reconstruct her life.

My return to La Floresta brought me back in contact with her. I found her in the corner of the terrace overhung with the red tiled roof. I heard the rich velvet tone of her voice as she stepped out of the house addressing and talking with her friends and as she drew up one of the cane chairs to sit with them here. I was lying in a cot in the soft sunshine next to them. I can almost see her now bending towards me, her dark hair flopped forwards, her warm smile melting with tenderness as she picks me up and lifts me out of the cot in her firm, strong arms. I see her again, more clearly this time, when I am a little older, a toddler on my feet. She is singing and teaching me some special songs. I still, even now, a lifetime gone by, recall their tunes and wording. She is getting me to repeat them after her and I sing, with my childish voice, the German sounds and their melodies without understanding where the words start or end, or their meaning. I can still hear her laughter and delight at how quickly I pick up her songs and remember them. Looking back on the enthusiasm with which she shared them with me and taught me to sing them, I now realise they must have been songs from her earlier, happier times back in Germany. With them, she was instilling in me the home she had lost and missed. I was not only her lively little girl, but also someone who would be with her always and share her losses and passions and pains, so she wouldn't be alone again. She was impressing on me those loved and familiar tunes, that they might remain engraved in my mind and I might carry them forward, along with her, as an insurance against forgetfulness, a part of herself she was entrusting me with, for its safekeeping.

I have also been back to Deià, in Mallorca, to recapture the landscape with its ancient olive groves and fig trees, cypresses and pines. To walk down Es Clot where I found the small stone house she had shared with Seppl, surrounded by the idyllic mountainous landscape she had loved and remembered from every corner of the earth where she was subsequently scattered. It is the last house on the steep winding track to the Cala below. Set back from the path and at the top of some stone steps, its arched entrance with a stone bench to one side, and a small square window above, identified it with the house in the fading black and white photographs in her album of Deià. The stone outhouse next to a rambling paddle cactus still stretches out on the other side of the steps, which continue uphill to the house at the back, hidden in the vegetation, on higher ground. Here is where my mother, Käte, experienced her happiest, carefree times. And here too, was where my own existence was just beginning. I can see her scrambling down through the olive groves and irregular terraces, climbing over the wooden fences that stop the goats and sheep straying from their turf, and balancing on the thick log stretched across the fast running stream that courses down alongside Es Clot from the village, finally making her way through the tall pines and past the delicious fruit bearing fig trees till the Cala suddenly appears round the last corner, the pebbled beach and blue emerald sea overlooked by the café on top of the rocks and stone wall.

As I retraced her walk, I stopped and stood now and then to look at some old olive trees, their creased and crinkled trunks twisted into swirling swollen joints, very much like the two olive trees in my mother's album, their lower trunks riven into two limb-like pedicles and their knotted contortions resembling a lovers' embrace.

These trees have been here for hundreds, maybe a thousand years, and my mother, then Käte, may have stood on this same spot to also marvel at their extraordinary forms, on her way down to the Cala in animated talk with Seppl. I see her strong lithe figure, tanned, lively and happy, manoeuvring through this landscape.

Photo of olive tree in Deià, in Käte's album, from early 1930s

Olive tree in Deià today

Today, Deià's beauty remains undimmed and is as arresting as ever, the magic light burnishing the Tramuntana mountain range that towers majestically in the background with its plethora of greens, rusts and buffs which permeate the landscape, interrupted with occasional splashes of bright red and magenta bougainvillea. Nature's rhythms and grandeur, here too, inspire awe and inner harmony.

Occupying the same space, at a different time and age. In some way, the olive trees – which have stood here since time immemorial and witnessed the passage of time – represent that mysterious point where those coordinates cross. If they could only speak – these venerated ancient symbols of the gods that crowned physical and spiritual beauty and achievement, and represented peace, glory, grace, life and fertility – if they could only speak and tell all that has passed during their existence, they might make known all that which forever will remain a mystery.

In similar vein, the unfinished portrait shall remain unpainted and unexplained and beyond our reach. And yet, understanding is to a large measure a relative thing: one moment we understand, and the next moment we have lost it. After close to a lifetime of misjudgements and misinterpretation, a few hours before she died, my mother said "I have understood". And in Kortokraks' portrait of me, one eye appears to be infused with the whole of my life and experience, and the other has been left blank, a green splodge left open for all that is to come.

Appendix

Käte's letters, 1939-40 (Excerpts)

Collioure, 2 February, 1939

... What I've lived through in the past few days here has been nearly worse than all the wartime I lived through in Spain. Thousands of refugees have arrived with nothing, nothing but the clothes on their backs, the poorest of the poor, university professors, manual labourers, children, arriving in small rowboats or on foot, chased by planes that shot at them with machine guns on their unhappy treks, through rain and snow, in the dark of night, starved almost to death. I was with the Consul at the border, saw things I will never forget, that still weigh on and oppress me all over again, I couldn't write, not knowing what to think or feel any longer. Dead children in bundles, dying soldiers from military hospitals. I have a houseful of people. We feel a sense of community as if we've known each other for ages, and since the Consul gave me a Spanish passport (saying I'd earned it more than most Spaniards, an exaggeration of course) I feel reborn, this time Spanish with my whole heart. And I cannot and do not wish to leave this, cannot contemplate a brand new life with entirely different people, with no relationships or bonds. I must stay here until we all know where to go, I will not and cannot now part from my friends. If we can't go back, I want to go with them to Mexico.

Foëgy, 27 July, 1939

My dearest Lottel, I just received your dear letter and want to reply straight away so it doesn't take even longer before we hear from each other. I have another five important letters to write today, but you come first, which is to say, I enjoy writing to you the most. And then of course I'm very intent that you don't worry about us too much, and secondly that you get better acquainted with my situation, which is not rosy indeed but has its pleasant moments. So, to begin with, we're doing well here. The Grandjean family is truly as friendly and generous as one could possibly expect, in fact better than one could expect. We lack for nothing that modest hearts, and especially stomachs and bodies could wish for. Miriam feels thoroughly at home here, and even though she is sleeping on a reclining chair and has an even more monotonous life than she had in Collioure, she is very well and in good spirits, which naturally has a strong and positive effect on my own situation. Now, that does not mean I would like this situation to go on forever and ever. I don't have a penny, for instance. I don't take anything from Lou anymore and even thinking of him gives me goose bumps.

Foëcy, October, 1939

My dear Lottel, I'm taking refuge in you a little because it is so hard to bear living so alone. It's one of those nights a person doesn't forget for a lifetime, nights so sad they leave their traces in the heart and soul. I don't even have the little sleeping Miriam here. She is staying with a kind elderly lady because I have got to work. At seven in the morning, I cycle for an hour (12 km) in the cold and usually rainy weather to work for some farmers. Ten hours for 25 francs a day. It's the grape harvest now, then comes the turnip harvest, then that will be over with and I'll have to find something else. I return at 7 pm exhausted to death, hardly able to stand. Back to my cold room. Nobody is waiting for me, no hot soup, no made bed. The mice in the cupboard have gnawed on the bread and the cheese. Then I peel off my wet clothes, wash myself and go to see Miriam, who is well cared for, more spoilt than suffering. But she says I make her sad. Then I feed her and tuck her in and go home and am too tired to light a fire and don't eat anything and get undressed and knit until my eyelids drop. Only I can't today because I'm too sad.

And tomorrow morning, while it's dark, I'll put those still-wet wrappings back on, climb onto my borrowed bicycle, and return to ten hours of work, stooping or squatting.

And I could probably cope with all that, even laugh at it, if you were here. Together. But to be this alone, it's too bleak. And Lou is in Paris and I have no clue what he is even up to there. He sends money very irregularly in very small amounts. Last month, 300 francs. Yesterday, 400. That's not even enough to cover Miriam's needs.

[…]

Our "house" is not in the Grandjeans' house. It's the house where Grandjean's father died a few weeks ago, a pauper's hut. Like a basement, with mice, dark and damp, but I've made it up very nice for myself and am glad to have an independent place where I can be alone.

I knit a lot and earn a bit of money from it, but no one can live off that because it's too poorly paid. It's just on the side.

[to her brother Fritz]

I would be very happy for Lottel if it still worked out with Australia. Even though it is far and there is no more prospect for me to be with her, she would at least start to feel at home or make a home for herself.

Write more often, especially if something changes with you. It's good to hear that Hansel receives regular news from Papi, although I think he can't really be doing so well.

Foëgy, 9 November, 1939

My dearest Lottel, Pevchen,[1]

Today I was overjoyed to receive a letter from Hansel and one in the same delivery from Fritzel, both letting me know that the two of you have at last succeeded in moving on from there. So, by this time, unless something else unforeseeable has come in the way, you are close to me. Or at least much closer. And no matter if we cannot see each other, that's a good feeling. And even when I think that we probably won't see one another for years to come, I'm still happy for you because I have quite a feeling that it's slightly better there than in this heinous world on this side. No matter what, you will see many beautiful things and I envy you the journey alone. Just to look around for a few weeks, a bit of joyful anticipation and a bit of trepidation and a bit of uncertainty but also confidence in one's heart, so to speak, that everything is pleasant and special for the two young chickens, an immensely rich experience. This will compensate for the many unhappy moments that your emigrant lives have brought. I'm so eager for your first impressions and your news. Wherever you dock, if the postage isn't too expensive, you must leave a few words for us. We are accompanying you all in our thoughts. But what good is that? We're staying here and "living" on. I haven't buried all hope, maybe one day something like a life will start for us, something to look forward to, something that occasionally makes you feel good and does not always bring pain and suffering. After all, I've adopted a new philosophy. Essentially this: Mutti[2] always said that one must look below oneself, in other words, imagine one could be worse off. Now I imagine I could have truly died and wished I could go back to love Miriam so she wouldn't have to suffer so much. So, I've come back and am living a little, just to avoid causing Miriam pain. That is all. And then it goes much better. Everything else is buried.

Lou was just here for a few days. Because it wasn't possible any other way, I'm accepting money from him again, so he's bought me again, so to speak, as Miriam's mother. Can't do anything else without asking him and have resigned myself to it. There will probably be more hours and weeks when that is very hard, but there is no other way. I can't live without his money now and, on the other hand, I can't demand for him to pay and then, one day when the mood strikes, get up and leave. But it fits with my philosophy quite well. So, I'm living somewhat better, materially speaking – Walter also sent me 100 francs today – and not working as much. Firstly because there isn't any work left and secondly because I couldn't stand it. I've even sent a parcel to A.'s brother today. Did you receive the last letter I sent to Haifa?

Miriam is sleeping sweetly beside me with her "Pepita" in her arms. Your doll, Ealein.[3] She's "reading" *Max and Moritz* with great interest and understanding and would love to meet them both (probably to give them a couple of cues for new pranks). But, at the end, when they've been ground up and eaten, she does say, as if redeemed: *C'est bien fait, ça.*[4] She's especially fond of Böck the tailor and always gazes intently and sympathetically at the page where he falls in cold water. – All of this is touching and I'm happy, very much so, when she's at my side. But always alone, with no-one to share in my happiness, what a mad life.

Hansel writes, I should send letters to poste restante in Genoa, and he'll keep you informed. And Fritzel on the *Adriatica*. I assume Fritzel is right because if he sends mail there and Hansel presumably also uses this address for you, this letter will also reach your hands, provided it even passes censorship these days.

So, you've made it to your beloved Italy after all. Don't take the farewell too hard. I know what it means to part from a country that is dear to your heart, all of it, its people, its art, its vegetation, everything. But I also know, or at least imagine, what a relief it must be to finally turn your back on a country that has brought you so much suffering … I assume that a letter from you to me is still on the way.

As for when we'll see one another, let's not waste too many words. I feel sorry about Papi because I have little hope there. Us, when we're old, even older. When Miriam is grown up. I have as my one soothing vision that we, Lottel – you and me as old ladies, if we are "fortunate" to reach that point – will live together, two old sisters with eccentric moods and habits, maybe with the *satis-facción* of having grandchildren somewhere in the world who send us letters now and then. Let's experience that together, at the very least, if the rest is not to be. And then we will say how nice such a life could have been.

So, look ahead, not behind, not below but yes also up above you, at night, with the starry sky over the sea and no people around, only the sounds of the ship and the water, the gently beating waves. Oh, how good that is, to be in such a quiet place so distant from so much sadness.

Goodbye. Everything I am and feel is travelling along with you,

Yours, Käte

Foëy, 18 May, 1940
(Addition handwritten above letter) Fritz rec'd. 21 May 40 – forwarded to Lottel on 22 May 40 with most heartfelt greetings. Unfortunately, no news from Hans yet
My dearest Lottel, Peetchen and Ealein,

This morning I received your letter, that is Lottel's, which Fritzel had sent on right away, from 20 April. I sadly never got to read the previous one with the first photos because Fritzel sent it to Holland before the big tragedy that has since unfolded there, and no more news is expected to make it out. – Over the past few

days, which have felt like years for all of us, I have had you especially in my thoughts. You have the same concerns as we do about
Hansel and the other side of the family, but in these hours, the
weight of our disconnection is so much heavier, like the state of
powerlessness we all find ourselves in. As you can see, I am in the
same situation here as ever, which has become even more
unpleasant these few days than before. But my only source of
suffering is to be alone during hours when the only salvation
would be a human soul who feels and understands the same
things. Lou is in Paris, writes occasionally, but he cannot do anything himself of course. It makes sense, now that our freedom
of movement is particularly limited. I am positive that the
moment Fritzel hears any word of Hansel or about the
Auerbachs, he will let you know by the fastest possible route. It's
all so grisly, but we hope the struggle won't be for nothing, that
the dragon will grow weary and dig his own grave. I'm sure that
by the time this letter reaches you, you will have received better
news. At any rate, we try to endure our fate and calmly face what
we cannot change. I am glad in the knowledge that you are far off
and if I knew a way to send Miriam to join you sooner or later, I
would be fully reassured and have no pain in my heart. Hardly any
pain.

What a strange impression they give, your photos, that sense
of peace, domesticity, garden, hopes and prospects. I am sooo
happy that you are doing well. If only you were spared from wor-
rying about us, you could be the happiest people ever – because
you've known enough of this side of the world to appreciate your
peace there. So be sensible. If everything goes pear-shaped here,
then don't take it more tragically than it is.

I'm glad that the green wool shawl is still coming in handy.
Who could have imagined it would accompany you all the way to
New Zealand and keep your back warm there? Does it snow

down there? Does it rain a lot this time of year? Here, according to the calendar, it's summer now, but two nice days were followed by three cold, rainy weeks. In any case, I still have my winter things on although they could use some airing out. The fact that you, my dear Ealein, are so concerned with helping Lottel and baking her cakes and making her surprises – yes, savour that now, all three of you. Living together is the only sensible source of joy. All the "big things" in life end in such dreadful disappointment and perhaps cause more calamity than they are worth. Yes, Peetchen, a vegetable garden and a harmonious life with those around us; everything else has a bitter reward in our times. But it seems to me that you've grasped this already and your ambitions are seeking grander avenues.

Congratulations on your American lodger, who hopefully won't bring any disappointment. May he be well-bred, rich, undemanding, and pleasant, in which case I wish him *a long and happy life* under your roof. Your dining-room corner fills me with wistfulness, not envy. If only once more in my life, to eat at a nicely set table, if possible with you!

Muckelchen[5] – she hasn't been called that in such a long time, but sadly you only know the Muckelchen from the old days – is a truly sturdy child, much like Ealein at that age: hefty, well-formed legs; good, solid tanned arms; a slim but not gaunt little body and very cheerful eyes. Unfortunately, she is the subject of far too many of my frequent sad spells, which I can't escape for all my best efforts. And she is rather sensitive now. We love each other beyond measure, which is only understandable. It would be better if we didn't, but many things would be better if they were different.

Yes, I hoped to move to Orléans, everything was ready, until the hardened heart of a bureaucrat – who it depended on not for everything, but for the main thing in those few critical days – prevented it once again. I haven't given up hope yet, but I understand that the men it depends on, who have been very friendly towards me, have more important work for the time being so I have got to wait. Patience, patience, I've never thought it possible that I could muster as much patience as I have required to cope here. But as you can see, I'm still here and still will be, and it goes on and on, and I'm not in despair. Sometime it seems like it, but then it keeps going on and on with renewed energy. That's called life and we keep hanging on and sometimes even laugh about it. So, you too should laugh and not fret. It's very nice that we all love each other so much and feel such pain and joy on each other's behalf. Maybe, maybe there will someday be a *happy ending*[1] in your little house, which I like so terribly much, with all the siblings and the nieces and nephews. Let's think about that instead of about what still needs to be survived before that day comes.

Hugging all three of you with my full heart,

Käte

[handwritten addition:] Miriam, who now speaks better French than Spanish, said this morning: *"Mama, tu sais, je n'aime pas mes grosses cuisses!"*[6] She is vain and would exchange her nicest toy for a tin brooch in a heartbeat. I wanted to send her to Lou in Paris for a few days, which would have been a joyful celebration for them both, but the war got in the way of that too.

Notes

1   Term of endearment for Peter, Lotte's son.
2   Mother.
3   Term of endearment for Eva, Lotte's daughter.
4   serves them right.
5   Term of endearment for Miriam, during the first years of her life.
6   "Mama, you know, I don't like my big thighs."

Translated from German by Jacob D. Schneider

Acknowledgements

I am deeply grateful for the backing and support I have received from many quarters, which have been conducive to the creation of *An Unfinished Portrait* – the readers of the book that precedes it, *My Innocent Absence*, having been among the most constant.

I shall forever remember with gratitude and friendship my late publisher, Gary Pulsifer, who encouraged me to write a sequel to *My Innocent Absence* and conveyed his enthusiasm with the first draft, and who, to my great sadness, did not live to see its completion. Gary's acute literary insight, integrity and taste, and his unwavering support and loyalty to his authors, is greatly missed, as is also his great sense of fun and joie de vivre. I should take this opportunity to also thank Danny Hahn and above all Daniela de Groote for their part in the publication of *My Innocent Absence*, and Angeline Rothermundt for her thoughtful and devoted editing assistance.

I would like to express my great appreciation to my publisher, Martin Rynja, with whom I have had highly engaging and enjoyable discussions over many cups of coffee on the making of *An Unfinished Portrait*, for his invaluable suggestions and guidance, as well as for his attentive dedication to the beautiful presentations of my books. Especial recognition in the gestation of *An Unfinished Portrait* belongs to my excellent editor Kate Murray-Browne for her admirably deft, insightful and keenly sensitive editing work and advice.

My heart-felt gratitude goes also to my Greek agent, Frankfurt Book Fair Fellow, and friend, Evangelia Avloniti, who secured the Greek publication of *My Innocent Absence* with the distinguished Kapon Editions, and who is always there for me when I require her assistance and advice. My great thanks are due also to Rachel Kapon for her thoughtful and thorough dedication to her very elegant Greek edition of the book.

For the making of *An Unfinished Portrait*, I am warmly grateful to Gary Soshat and Maria Roldan Valiente, who helped me in my search for and invited me to stay at my first home in La Floresta, near Barcelona, where the first chapter of the book took shape, and to the house's present proprietors, Dino Ibanez and Dolors Juncosa, who shared with me its fascinating story, as well as their friendship and home in Palma Mallorca. A great thank you to William and Lucia Graves, who generously invited me and went over that period of their father's early years in Deià and my mother's photographs of the time, and assisted me with my research. I would also like to express my gratitude to Maria Angels Cuadras Avellana, of San Cugat del Vallès, who showed my mother's early photographs and presented *My Innocent Absence* in pride of place, in her great, memorable exhibition of historical photographs of La Floresta.

The Spanish film historian, Pau Martinez Muñoz's warm hospitality in her flat in Barcelona, where she showed me her copies of my father's films of the Spanish Civil War and spoke to me of her research into them, was much appreciated. Thank you also to Leonora Moreleón, who presented my autobiography and my father's films in Athens, and to Vincenza Fava, for all her thought and labour in preparation of an evening of talks and readings, including her translation of my writing, to a packed audience, facilitated by the librarian, Enio Staccini, and with Anna Rita and Pino Brachetti's contribution, presided by the Mayor, Fabio Bartolacci, in Santa Croce, Tuscania. Wholehearted thanks also to Claudio Patrizi, who is mounting a Kortokraks exhibition and launching my books in the forthcoming months.

My writing and difficult development of the complex story I wished to covey and share with readers, has been much assisted by the thoughtful and constructive comments from generous friends and family. I am much indebted to my old school friend from my New Zealand years, with whom I have recently been reunited,

Sally Page, for her thorough reading and helpful suggestions of my manuscript in the making, as also from my life-long friend and colleague dating from our medical school days, Barry Cant, whose observations from a neurologist's viewpoint are always penetrating and frank. Guy Slater examined my writing with the rigour he is accustomed to in his theatre direction, and Athens resident and friend Jonathan Sim's rich literary background, and Deborah Shepard's memoir mentoring experience in New Zealand, added to the broad range of helpful comments. I also relished art specialist and writer Richard Aronowitz's thoughtful response. And to these I should like to add the backing and assistance from James Greene, Wendy Savage, Enid Richemont, Carol Shand, Leona Fay, Angela Kiossoglou, Sonaid Sinclair, Nicole Mihaud, Erika Tophoven, and Jon and Marion Boock.

I am grateful also to my sister Evelyn Frank and my younger daughter Anna Gunin, the first a musician and the second a translator of Russian literature, for their perceptive and considered comments, and to my older daughter Rebekah Kortokraks who used her imaginative graphic design skills for my website, and my cousin Noam Leshem who kindly helps me with its updating.

Finally, and by no means least, I am deeply indebted to Rebecca Tansley, who organized my last reading circuit in New Zealand of *My Innocent Absence* and has now undertaken to help create and launch her beautiful Special Edition of *An Unfinished Portrait* from Auckland in the North Island to Dunedin in the South, for her painstaking dedication, even as she is preparing to present her own film in California and Rome. And to Maria Collins who invited me to talk to the University of the Third Age in Auckland where I was treated to a moving reception from an enthusiastic audience, and to Brigid Denniston who is now taking me to beautiful Queenstown for a similar presentation, and to Liz Riley for her part in it, and so many others who have movingly supported, helped, responded and encouraged me throughout, and whom I shall forever cherish.